ANNOTA
TEACHER'S B

READING
COMPREHENSION
WORKSHOP
CROSSROADS

Globe
Fearon

GLOBE FEARON EDUCATIONAL PUBLISHER
Upper Saddle River, New Jersey
www.globefearon.com

Executive Editor: Virginia Seeley
Senior Editor: Bernice Golden
Editor: Lynn W. Kloss
Editorial Assistant: Roger Weisman
Product Development: Book Production Systems
Art Director: Nancy Sharkey
Production Manager: Penny Gibson
Production Editors: Nicole Cypher, Eric Dawson
Marketing Manager: Sandra Hutchison
Photo Research: Jenifer Hixson
Electronic Page Production: Siren Design
Cover Design: Carol Anson
Cover Illustration: Jennifer Bolten

Globe Fearon Educational Publisher wishes to thank the following copyright owners for permission to reproduce copyrighted selections in this book: **Atheneum Publishers**, for Andrew A. Rooney, "Advertising," from *The Most of Andy Rooney*, originally published in *A Few Minutes with Andy Rooney*, copyright 1966, 1968, 1969, 1971, 1974, 1975, 1976, 1977, 1978, 1979, 1980 by CBS, Inc., copyright 1981 by Essay Productions, Inc.; **Bilingual Press / Editorial Bilingue**, Arizona State University, Tempe, AZ, for Marta Salinas, "The Scholarship Jacket," edited from *Nosotras: Latina Literature Today* by Maria del Carmen Boza, Beverly Silva, and Carmen Valle (1986); **HarperCollins Publishers**, for Huynh Quang Nhuong, excerpt from *The Land I Lost*, copyright 1982 by Huynh Quang Nhuong; **Hodder & Stoughton Ltd.**, for Sidney Poitier, excerpt from *This Life*, copyright 1980 by Sidney Poitier; **Alfred A. Knopf, Inc.**, for Sidney Poitier, excerpt from *This Life*, copyright 1980 by Sidney Poitier; **Philomel Books, an imprint of G. P. Putnam's Sons**, for Judith Gorog, "Prosperity," from *Three Dreams and a Nightmare and Other Tales of the Dark*, text copyright 1988 by Judith Gorog. Globe Fearon has executed a reasonable and concerted effort to contact the author of "The Cave" by Enrique Jaramillo Levi, published in *Where Angels Glide at Dawn: New Stories from Latin America*, text copyright (c) 1990 by Lori Carlson and Cynthia Ventura. Globe Fearon eagerly invites any persons knowledgeable about the whereabouts of this author to contact Globe Fearon to arrange for the customary publishing transactions.

Globe Fearon Educational Publisher wishes to thank the following copyright owners for permission to reproduce illustrations and photographs in this book: **p. 10**: Illustration of a wagon in moonlight by Kenneth Spengler; **p. 46**: Photograph of Xuxa, Courtesy MTM Entertainment Co.; **p. 49**: Photograph of Billy Mills, Courtesy Billy Mills; **p. 64**: Photograph of Sidney Poitier, Wide World Photos; **p. 66**: Illustration of rice field in Vietnam by David Tamura; **p. 97**: Photograph of teens in a classroom, Elizabeth Crews, Stock Boston; **p. 114**: Illustration of garbage truck by Kenneth Spengler.

Printed in the United States of America   3 4 5 6 7 8 9 10

ISBN: 0-835-90581-0

GLOBE FEARON EDUCATIONAL PUBLISHER
Upper Saddle River, New Jersey
www.globefearon.com

CONTENTS in Order of Skill Presentation

OVERVIEW

The goal of *Reading Comprehension Workshop* is to help students become skilled **active readers**. As they complete the lessons, students interact with the text by applying skills and strategies. Each *Workshop* lesson helps students become aware of the natural reading process by learning what skilled readers "see" as they read for understanding. **Skills and strategies** that are central to the *Workshop*, such as Cause and Effect, Main Idea and Details, and Author's Purpose, are described in a way that clarifies why and how they can be used to read actively. A graphic organizer visually demonstrates each skill and strategy.

Reading Comprehension Workshop develops **critical thinking skills** that help students make connections between old ideas and new. It shows them how to find new information and to utilize prior knowledge. Through the *Workshop*, students discover how to respond to literature. They respond by discussing and writing about their thoughts and ideas as well as how the text makes them feel. Through active participation, students learn to slow down the reading process so that they can see it "one frame at a time." Students learn to take control of their reading by rereading for clarification, visualizing for understanding, and responding to what they read.

The **multicultural literature** selected for the *Workshop* is original and not adapted. The below-grade reading levels and high-interest content of the selections are appropriate for improving readers and for **ESL/LEP** students. Fiction and nonfiction genres are equally represented; all literature within a unit is taken from the same genre. In addition, units are paired by genre.

Reading Comprehension Workshop also prepares students for state **reading proficiency tests**. All skills included in the workshop reflect state standards in the language arts and reflect testing terminology, format, and procedures.

A Walk Through a Unit

As you glance at the table of contents, you will notice that the student text is divided into units. Each unit begins with a **Unit Opener** and contains two lessons and two multicultural literature selections. As you page through a unit, you will see that the lessons follow a logical plan. This plan provides a page in each lesson for **Introducing, Practicing,** and **Applying** each of the lesson skills before the literature selections, and **Reviewing** and **Testing** after the selections.

As you can see, a **Lesson Bar** (on page 2, for example) appears across the top of each lesson page. Notice how the lesson bar shows the student the page on which each part of the lesson appears. Note that the words *Introducing, Practicing, Applying, Reviewing,* and *Testing* match the sequence of lesson components mentioned above.

Arrow Guides also direct students through each unit. If you turn to page 4 of the student text (the first Applying page of the book), you will see an arrow, which will direct you to the Reviewing page for that lesson. Arrow guides direct students from lesson pages to selection pages.

The two literature selections within each unit are adjacent to one another. The **Model Selection**—the first of the two literary works—is used to introduce and provide practice for both lessons in the unit. The **Review Selection** is used to review and test the skills and strategies in both lessons.

Workshop Features

Unit Openers Openers introduce the genre and encourage students to become active readers. You can use this feature to let students know why the skills and strategies presented in the unit are useful and to discuss how culture is reflected in the genre of the unit's selections. You can also use this feature to help students make connections between the reader's response to literature and the writing of sidenotes.

Level	Title	Reading/ Interest Level	Genres
Book 1	Insights	3/6	Folktales, Myths, Short Stories, Poems, Articles
Book 2	Crossroads	4/7	Short Stories, Biographies, Autobiographies, Speeches, Essays
Book 3	Reflections	5/8	Short Stories, Articles, Essays, Poems
Book 4	Momentum	6/9	Novel Excerpts, Newspaper Articles, Magazine Articles, Encyclopedia Articles, How-to Articles, Poems
Book 5	Perspective	7/10	Short Stories, Editorials, Plays, Humorous Essays, Persuasive Essays
Book 6	Spectrum	8/11	Novel Excerpts, Short Stories, Letters, Advertorials, Encyclopedia Articles, Poems, Songs, Reference Articles, Encyclopedia Articles

Model and Review Selections The Model and Review Selections were carefully selected for their diverse cultural voices. Since the interest level of the literature is high, you can use it to motivate students to read, discuss key issues, and apply the skills and strategies. The nonfiction fosters a critical view of ideas; the fiction encourages a comparison of new and known ideas.

Sidenotes Sidenotes show how one reader responded while reading. They also model how that reader applied the lesson skill and strategy to the selection. Space is provided in the margins for students to write their own sidenotes for both the Model Selection and the Review Selection. Students might need several practice sessions writing sidenotes as they actively become involved in the reading process.

Graphic Organizers In every lesson, the Introducing page presents a graphic organizer that shows students the process of applying the skill and strategy being taught. Students use the graphic organizers to apply the skill and strategy to the unit selections.

Writing Activities Students are given many opportunities to increase their comprehension skills through writing. A writing prompt appears in Section B of every Practicing, Applying, Reviewing, and Testing page. These writing activities develop the students' critical thinking skills and allow them to express their own ideas about key issues presented in the selections. Brief writing activities appear on every Introducing page, allowing students to respond to the sidenotes. In addition, students comment in writing about their answers to test items.

Assessment The two **Testing** pages in each unit and the **Book Tests** at the end of the book are geared toward the state proficiency tests. Various testing formats are included: cloze, multiple choice, true-false, and fill-in-the-blanks. In addition, more than one answer is sometimes correct. Students must support each answer with a written statement explaining their reasoning.

ANNOTATED TEACHER'S EDITION

The *Reading Comprehension Workshop Annotated Teacher's Edition* provides you with suggested student answers and teacher annotations at point of use. It also gives you options for extending the lesson.

Student Answers

Many of the questions in the program are open-ended, allowing for a range of answers. The same is true of the writing activities and the graphic organizers. However, the *Workshop ATE* provides model answers and suggestions for responses to questions, writing activities, and graphic organizers. Use the modeled Student Answers to assess students' responses. Keep in mind that a student's answer is acceptable if he/she can support it with adequate evidence from the selection or from prior knowledge.

Teacher Annotations

Three types of Teacher Annotations, which are positioned in the margins, provide you with a variety of support systems. General Annotations appear throughout the program. Page-Specific Annotations appear on the same pages throughout the ATE. Assessment Annotations suggest alternative ways to assess students' work.

General Annotations General Annotations that provide suggestions for developing the language skills of students acquiring English appear as **ESL/LEP** annotations. These annotations focus on dramatization, visual interpretation, and oral language development. **Peer Sharing, Individualized Learning**, and **Cooperative Learning** annotations provide recommendations for grouping students. **Writing Process** and **Conferencing** annotations provide suggestions for expanding student writing and guiding students' responses to each other's writing.

Page-Specific Annotations Each ATE Introducing page begins with the **Lesson Objective**, shows you an approach for **Modeling the Strategy**, and gives pointers for **Managing the Lesson**.

The Practicing page of the ATE clarifies the **Purpose** of the page and explains how students can use the strategy in the graphic organizer to complete the page.

The ATE Applying page provides suggestions for **Applying the Skill to Other Media, Applying the Skill to Everyday Reading**, or **Applying the Skill to Other Disciplines.**

Annotations on the first Literature page include **Preteaching Vocabulary, Motivating Question, Accessing Prior Knowledge**, or **Making Predictions**, each of which promotes student interaction with the text before reading. While the student is reading, annotations highlight **Additional Skills, Cultural Awareness**, and **Meeting Individual Needs**, each of which focus on the special needs of students. In addition, a **Clarification** annotation offers students the opportunity to clarify their understanding of the selection.

Annotations that provide **Response Clues** suggest ways that students might apply the skill to the selection through writing sidenotes and marking text by circling, underlining, and drawing arrows. Note that the Response Clues and marks within the text are suggestions, since there are no required responses.

The annotations on the Reviewing page give suggestions for **Reviewing the Strategy**. Annotations on the **Testing** page include **Test-Taking Hints**.

Assessment Annotations Assessment Annotations provide alternative guidelines to measure student learning. These include **Student Self-Assessment, Assessing Cooperative Work**, and **Assessing Student Writing**.

LIST OF WORKSHOP SKILLS

Insights, Crossroads, Reflections

UO = Unit Opener	L = Lesson	Boldface = Lesson Title in *Crossroads*		

COMPREHENSION	Book 1 Insights	Book 2 Crossroads	Book 3 Reflections
Drawing conclusions	UO2, L3		UO2, L3
Cause and effect	UO2, L4	UO4, L8	UO6, L11
Predicting outcomes	OU3, 4, L7		
Making inferences		UO2, L3	
Sequence		UO4, L7	
Main idea and details		UO7, L14	UO4, L8
Compare and contrast			UO4, 6, L7
Fact and opinion		UO6, L11,12	
CRITICAL THINKING			
Responding to various forms of literature	applied throughout the series		
Using prior knowledge/personal experience			
• to understand what is read	UO1,4,7	UO2,5,6	UO2,4
• to predict outcomes	L7		UO3
• to make inferences		L3	
Key questions	UO7, L14		
Summarizing	L14	UO7	
Making judgments		UO6, L12	
Visualizing characters and settings			UO1
Analyzing writer's argument			UO4
Evaluating similarities and differences			L7
GENRE AND AUTHOR'S CRAFT			
Recognizing fantasy		UO1, L1	
Point of view	UO3, L5		
Sound, form, and meaning	UO5, L9		
Subject of a poem	UO6, L11		
Imagery	UO6, L12		
Reading			
• articles	UO7, L13		
• essays		UO7, L13	

• folktales and myths	UO1, L1		
• nonfiction			UO3, L5,7
• **speeches**		UO5, L9	
Plot		UO2, L4	UO1, L1
Author's viewpoint		UO3, L5	UO5, L9
Author's purpose		UO6, L11,13	L9
Recognizing persuasive language		UO6, L11	
Story conflict			UO1, L1
Problem and solution			UO2, L4
Speaker of a poem			UO7, L13
Mood			UO7, L14
APPRECIATING DIVERSITY			
Recognizing commonalties among cultures	UO3	UO1	UO7
Recognizing similarities and differences among all people	UO4,5, L8	UO4	UO1,5, L12
Clues to culture	UO4, L8		
Appreciating the diversity of a multicultural society	UO7	UO3	
Appreciating one's heritage		L14	L6
Developing understanding and tolerating differences			UO1
Recognizing the diversity within a culture		UO7	UO2,5
Cultural context			UO6, L12
VOCABULARY			
Pronouns	UO1, L2		
Context clues	UO3, L6	UO3, L6	UO1,5 L2,10,11
Classifying words	L10, L12		
Base words and affixes		UO1, L2	
• **Prefixes**		UO1, L2	
• **Suffixes**		UO1, L2	
Multiple meaning words		UO3, L6	
Synonyms and antonyms		UO5, L10	L10
Identifying words			
• that signal cause-effect relationships			L11
• that signal sequences		L7	
Idioms			UO1, L2
Key words			UO3, L6

CONTENTS by Cultural Group

This list shows the cultural background of the authors whose selections appear in *Insights, Crossroads,* and *Reflections.*

Name ______________________________ Date ____________

Recognizing Fantasy: Use story details to decide whether you are reading a fantasy or a realistic story. Then organize your thoughts by writing your findings on the chart below.

Question	Yes	No	Look back at details	Confirm
Are some of the places unlike places in the real world?	☐	☐		Fantasy or Realistic Story?
Do unusual events occur?	☐	☐		
Do some characters have traits or abilities that real people don't have?	☐	☐		

Name ______________________________ Date ____________

Plot Development: Make notes about the plot as you read the story. Fill in the chart below to keep track of the story's events.

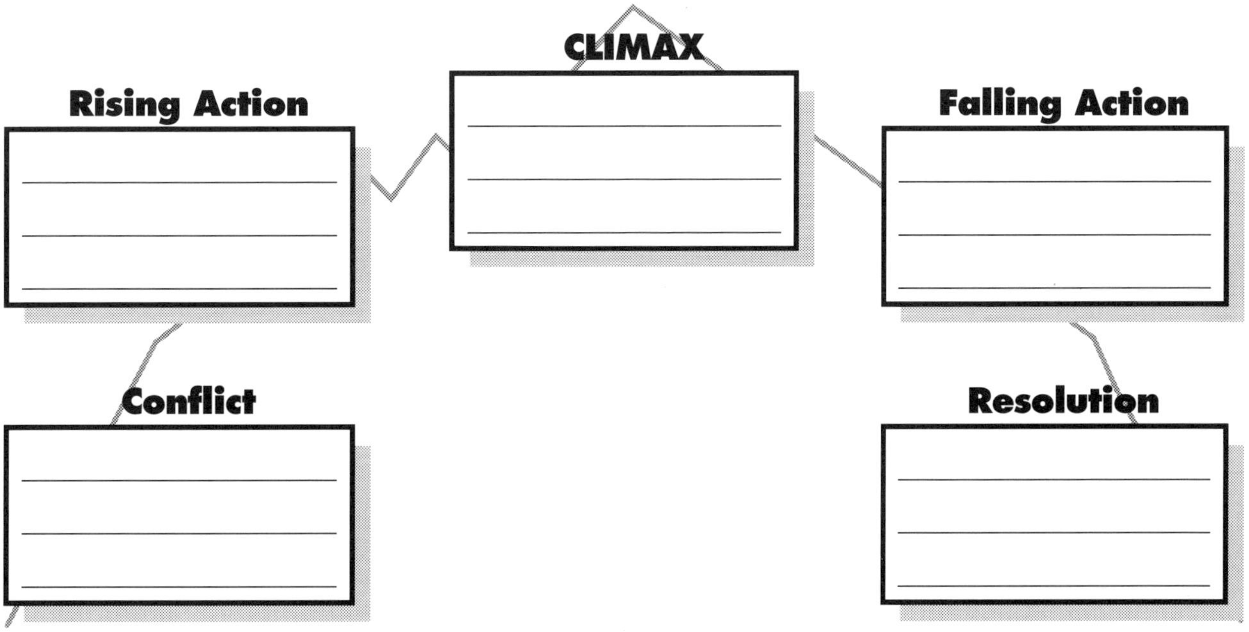
CLIMAX
Rising Action
Falling Action
Conflict
Resolution

Copyright © Globe Fearon Educational Publisher. All rights reserved.

Name _____ Date _____

Making Inferences: Combine selection details with what you already know to make inferences. Write your responses for one inference in the puzzle pieces below.

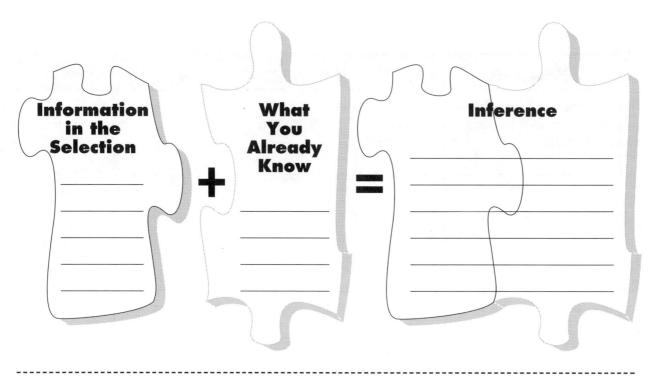

- -

Name _____ Date _____

Cause and Effect: As you read the selection, circle the causes you find and draw arrows to their effects. Then use your findings in the chart below to show how one action can influence another event.

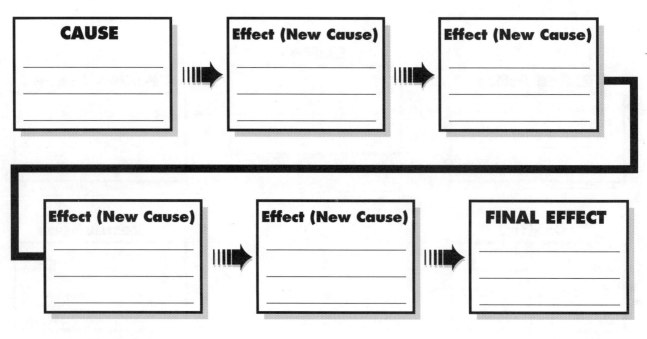

Name _____ Date_____

Making Judgments: Circle the facts and underline the opinions you found in the selection. Combine this information with what you already know to make a judgment.

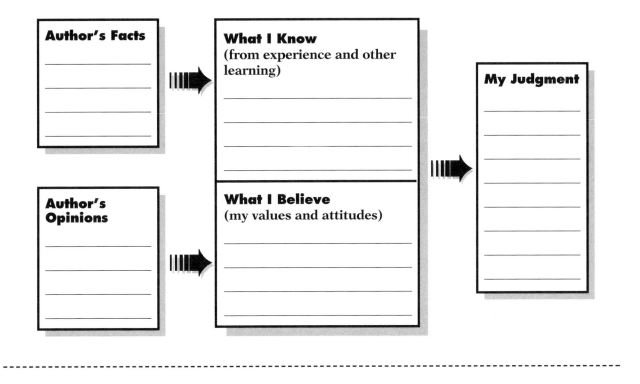

- -

Name _____ Date_____

Main Idea and Details: After reading the selection, underline the main idea and circle the details that support it. Record your findings on the wheel below.

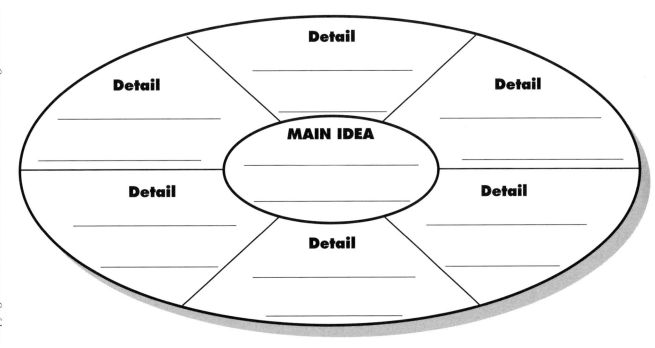

T 13

Name _____ **Date**_____

Author's Viewpoint: Think about the facts, quotes, and dialogue that the author uses to describe the subject. Use this information on the wheel below to find the author's viewpoint.

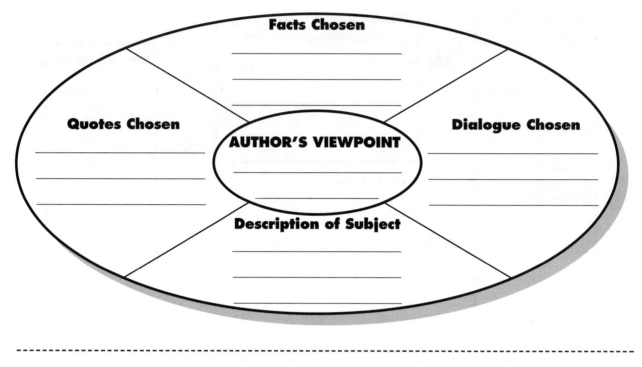

- -

Name _____ **Date**_____

Synonyms and Antonyms: Use a dictionary and a thesaurus to help you find synonyms and antonyms for a word in the selection. Record your findings on the chart below.

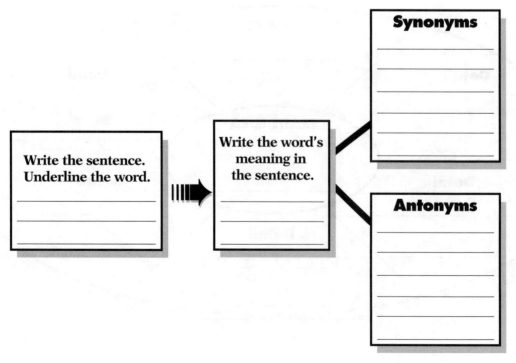

T 14

Name _____ **Date**_____

Author's Purpose: Underline the facts, opinions, and the persuasive language that are clues to the author's purpose. Analyze this information by filling out the chart below.

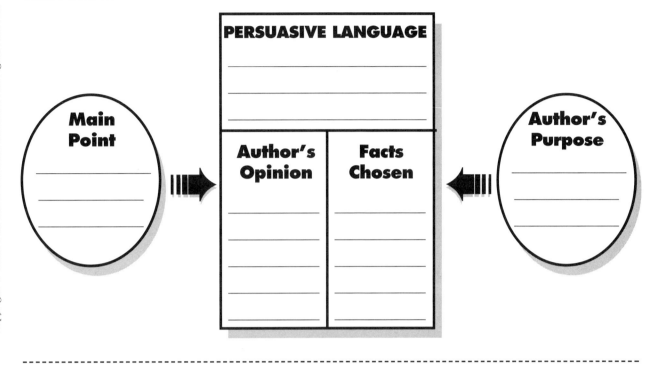

Name _____ **Date**_____

Multiple Meaning Words: Use a dictionary to help you determine the correct meaning for a multiple meaning word in a sentence. Summarize your findings on the diagram below.

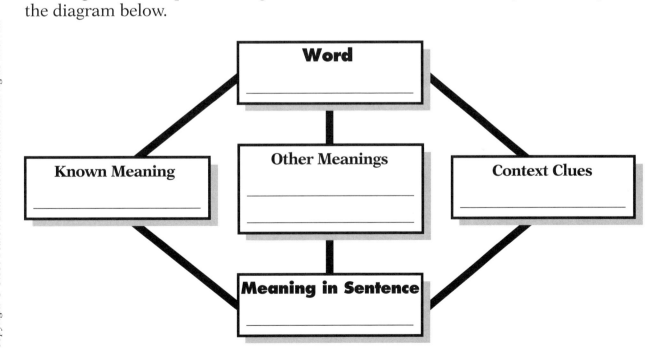

Name _____ Date _____

Sequence: Write notes about the order in which events are presented. Use these notes to analyze the selection's action or arguments on the sequence chain below.

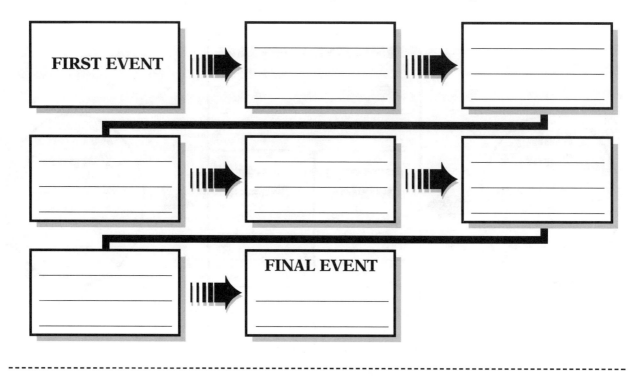

- -

Name _____ Date _____

Structure of Speeches: Circle the topic and make notes about the details and persuasive language that support it. Use your findings on the chart below to clarify the structure of the speech.

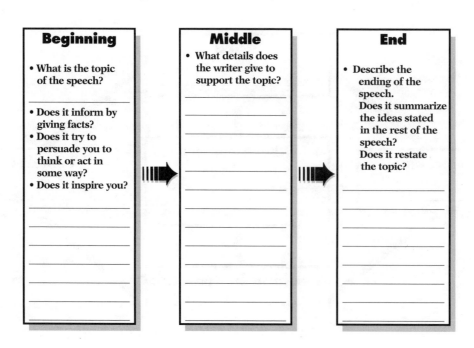

Unit ONE

BECOMING AN ACTIVE READER

Good readers are active readers. They ask questions about what is happening in a **fantasy** story. Then they compare the story's events and characters to events and people they know about.

Using Skills and Strategies

Recognizing fantastic details will help you determine whether a story is a **fantasy** or a **realistic story**. As you read, you may ask: Could this really happen? Can people do this in real life?

Finding **base words** and their **affixes**, or suffixes and prefixes, can help you figure out the meaning of unfamiliar words. You may ask: What part of the word carries its main meaning? Is there a prefix? How does the prefix change the word's meaning? Is there a suffix? How does the suffix change the word's meaning?

In this unit, learning to recognize **fantasy** and to define words by using **base words** and **affixes** will help you read stories actively.

The Fantasy: The Writer's Voice

Fantasies may take place hundreds of years in the future, in another galaxy, or in a land with no humans. They may be set in a world that seems familiar until something impossible happens. In most cultures, fantasies tell people something about themselves. Even if none of the characters or situations seems real, there is always something about the story that is familiar. In this way, storytellers and writers tell people something about themselves or their culture.

Responding to Stories

Good readers often feel as if they are involved in fantasies. They may wish they could warn story characters of danger or give them advice. Write your reactions in the margins as you read "Prosperity" and "The Cave." Use these sidenotes as you discuss the stories with your classmates.

Unit Enrichment: Ask students to imagine that the orphaned boy and the young adventurer in "Prosperity" and "The Cave" have become pen pals. Have partners pretend to be one of these characters and write letters back and forth each day for a week. Their letters should recount each character's thoughts and experiences.

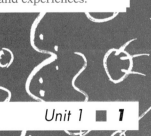

Recognizing Fantasy

Lesson Objective: To distinguish between realistic stories and fantasies by evaluating details in the short stories "Prosperity" and "The Cave."

ESL/LEP: Show pictures of fantastic scenes and invite students to describe what they see.

Introducing Strategies

When you read a story, you set out on a journey to a world created by the author. In a **realistic story**, the author creates a real world similar to the one you live in. The characters are like people you know, and they do things real people can do. In another type of story, a **fantasy**, the author adds details that could not happen in the real world. For example, buildings might vanish and reappear and characters may change into machines. These strange details in a fantasy are called **fantastic** details.

The checklist below can help you figure out whether a story is a **fantasy** or a **realistic story**.

Modeling the Strategy: Read aloud a passage from a fantasy to model identifying realistic and fantastic details. Refer to the steps in the chart. After completing the page, use the Reproducible Activity Master on page T11 of the ATE to help students apply the strategy to "Prosperity."

Question	Yes	No	Look back at details	Confirm
Are some of the places unlike places in the real world?			Write details about the places in the story.	Fantasy or Realistic Story?
Do unusual events occur?			Write details about events in the story.	
Do some characters have traits or abilities that real people don't have?			Write details about characters in the story.	

Reading the Short Story

Managing the Lesson: Remind students to use the sidenotes on pages 8-9 to model the process of active reading and to help them answer questions 1 and 2.

Read "Prosperity" on pages 8-11 and the sidenotes on pages 8-9. These sidenotes show what one good reader noticed about realistic and fantastic details in the story. After you have finished reading, answer the questions below.

1. List two realistic details pointed out in the sidenotes.

Students might suggest: The boy is waiting for a wagon ride, he is hungry and cold,

an old man stops to give him a ride.

2. List two fantastic details pointed out in the sidenotes.

Students might suggest: The pot of stew stays full even though the boy eats from it,

the man says he will help mend a tear in the fabric of time.

Practicing Recognizing Fantasy

A. In each pair of statements below, there is one realistic detail and one fantastic detail. Circle the letter of the fantastic detail and explain your choice on the lines that follow it.

1. a. The man is helping mend the tear in the fabric of time.
   b. The man stopped to give the boy a ride in the wagon.

   Time is not something you can see and touch, so it couldn't really have a tear in it.

2. a. The horse only appears to be old; he never tires.
   b. The horse, freshly groomed, was pale and shimmering.

   All real people and animals get tired sometimes.

3. a. The stewpot was in the back of the wagon.
   b. The boy ate a lot, but the stewpot was never empty.

   Eating from a real pot will eventually empty it.

4. a. During the seven years, the young man prospered.
   b. After seven years, the old man looked the same age.

   People look older after seven years have passed.

B. What adventures do you think the young man will have during his seven years? Write a paragraph that tells about one adventure. Underline the fantastic details in your paragraph.

Remind students to include some characters, places, or events that could not appear

in realistic stories. They may include animals that talk, strange ways of getting food

and water, and secrets for not aging.

Purpose: The purpose of this page is to help students practice distinguishing between realistic stories and fantasies. Questions reflect the strategy illustrated in the chart on the **Introducing** page.

Peer Sharing: Have students complete Section A with a classmate. Partners may rewrite their choices to make them realistic.

ESL/LEP: Although most of the vocabulary in this story is simple, the fantasy aspect could be confusing to students. Have them work with a partner to determine which events could happen and which could not. Partners might discuss, pantomime, or draw the images presented.

Conferencing: Have students conference with a peer to identify the fantastic details in each other's paragraphs.

Applying *Recognizing Fantasy*

A. Read the excerpt below from the short story "A Huge Black Umbrella," by Marjorie Agosín. In this story, Delfina Nahuenhual is a mysterious woman who works as a nanny, taking care of children. The story is told by one of these children who is now grown up. When you've finished reading, complete the activity that follows.

So I never did meet the person to whom Delfina Nahuenhual wrote her letters nor learned why she spent her sleepless nights writing them. I only learned that he was a leper on Easter Island, that he was still alive and, perhaps, still reads the letters, the dreams of love Delfina Nahuenhual had each night. When I returned home, I knew at last that Delfina Nahuenhual was content, because when I looked up, as she had taught me to do, I saw a huge black umbrella hovering in the cloudy sky.

Decide whether each item below is a realistic or a fantastic detail. Write the word *realistic* or *fantastic* on the line below each item and explain your choice.

1. a leper, a person who suffers from the disease leprosy

realistic: leprosy is a real disease

2. Easter Island, an island in the southern Pacific Ocean

realistic: Easter Island is a real place

3. a huge black umbrella hanging in the sky

fantastic: an umbrella can't hang alone in the sky

B. Choose a real place and write three details that describe it. Then write three more details that you could add to the description that would make it fantastic.

Make sure that students are able to differentiate between the realistic and fantastic details they use in their descriptions. You may wish to have them write "R" above realistic details and "F" above fantastic details. Students might write about school, home, neighborhoods, or nature.

Applying the Skill to Other Media: Ask students to discuss movies, plays, or TV shows that are fantasies. Have them give details about fantastic characters, settings, and events.

Individualized Learning: Have students complete Section A independently. Make sure that they have provided explanations that support their responses.

Peer Sharing: Have students complete Section B independently, then share what they have written with a partner. Students should make sure that their partner has included three realistic and three fantastic details.

Writing Process: Students might expand their description into a total writing process activity.

To review
page 15

Base Words and Affixes

Introducing Strategies

When good readers find an unfamiliar word, they try to figure out its meaning by breaking the word into parts. A **base word** carries the word's main meaning. An **affix** is a group of letters that changes the meaning of the base word. Two types of affixes are **prefixes** and **suffixes**. For example, suppose you read the sentence *The train derailed* and did not know the meaning of *derailed*. By breaking the word into parts, you would learn that the prefix *de-* means "away from," the base word *rail* means "the train's track," and the suffix *-ed* shows that something happened in the past. *Derailed*, then, means "off the track."

This chart shows how to figure out a word's meaning.

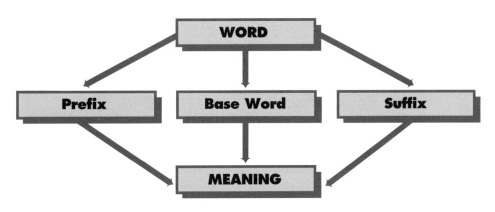

Reading the Short Story

Reread "Prosperity" on pages 8-11. As you read, underline words that contain a base word with a prefix, suffix, or both. Use this information to complete the items below.

1. List and define two words you found that have prefixes.

Students might suggest: *unhitched*: freed from being fastened and *unharnessed*: freed

from being connected to a wagon.

2. List and define two words you found that have suffixes.

Students might suggest: *argument*: the act of quarreling or disagreeing and *greedy*: in

a way that shows the desire to take all one can.

Lesson Objective: To find the meaning of unfamiliar words by identifying base words and affixes in the short stories "Prosperity" and "The Cave."

ESL/LEP: Review with students the use of suffixes that change tenses from singular to plural and from present to past.

Modeling the Strategy: Read aloud a news article to model breaking an unfamiliar word into parts. Refer to the parts of the diagram.

Managing the Lesson: Remind students that they may use the base words with affixes they have underlined in the story to help them answer questions 1 and 2.

Practicing Base Words and Affixes

A. Read the sentences below and the information about affixes. Then write the base word and the meaning of the boldfaced word.

1. "He was very old, his face **ashen** in the moonlight."

    -en is a suffix meaning "resembling"

base word: *ash*; meaning: resembling ashes, or what is left after something is burned

2. "The horse had been **unhitched** from the wagon."

    un- is a prefix meaning "the opposite of"

    -ed is a suffix showing past tense

base word: *hitch*; meaning: having been freed from a harness

3. "The boy **unharnessed** the horse."

    un- is a prefix meaning "the opposite of"

base word: *harness*; meaning: having had gear removed that attached a horse

to a wagon

4. "Only from the **orphanage**."

    -age is a suffix meaning "place or house of"

base word: *orphan*; meaning: a place where children live who have no parents

5. "'**Prosperity**?' the boy repeated, a bit disappointed."

    -ity is a suffix meaning "state or quality"

base word: *prosper*; meaning: state of being successful

B. Write sentences with words that contain these prefixes: *un-, non-, pre-*. Then write sentences with words that contain these suffixes: *-tion, -ly, -ment*.

Students might use the following words: *untie, unfasten; nonsmoking, nonconformist;*

preview, preheat; ambition, subtraction; quickly, slowly; entertainment, treatment. Make

sure students have spelled these words correctly and used them appropriately.

Purpose: The purpose of this page is to help students practice finding the meaning of unfamiliar words by breaking them into base words and affixes. Questions reflect the strategy illustrated in the diagram on the **Introducing** page.

Peer Sharing: Have students complete Section A independently. When they are finished, have them work with a partner to list three additional words that contain each affix.

Cooperative Learning: Have students complete Section B in groups of three. One student should be the reader, another the moderator, and the third the recorder.

Applying Base Words and Affixes

A. Read the excerpt from Marjorie Agosín's short story, "A Huge Black Umbrella." Then answer the questions that follow it.

> *For many years, I kept her little pot like a precious secret, a kind of <u>magical</u> lamp in which my <u>childhood</u> was captured. When I wanted to remember her, I rubbed the pot, I smelled it, and all my fears, including my fear of <u>darkness</u>, vanished.*

1. What are the base word and suffix of *magical*? What does the whole word mean?

magic and *-al*: having a mysterious power or influence

2. What are the base word and suffix of *childhood*? How does the suffix change the meaning of the base word?

child and *-hood*: the suffix changes the meaning from "a young boy or girl" to "a time

during which one is a young boy or girl"

3. What are the base word and suffix of *darkness*? How does the suffix change the meaning of the base word?

dark and *-ness*: the suffix changes the meaning from "without light" to "a state of

being without light"

B. Write three sentences of your own. Include one or more base words with affixes in each sentence. Try to add both a prefix and a suffix to at least one base word.

Make sure that students have used both prefixes and suffixes in their sentences and

that they have used at least one word with both types of affixes.

_____

_____

_____

_____

_____

_____

_____

Applying the Skill to Everyday Reading: Students can practice breaking unfamiliar words into base words and affixes as they read magazines and newspapers.

ESL/LEP: Clarify the meaning of the passage by having volunteers take turns acting out the scene presented. Follow this with a brief discussion of some of the phrases that cannot be easily demonstrated, such as *precious secret* and the idiom *my childhood was captured.*

Peer Sharing: Have students complete Section A with a classmate. Both students should be able to explain their choices.

Individualized Learning: Have students complete Section B independently. Have them circle the words with affixes they have used.

To review
↓
page
17

Preteaching Vocabulary:
You may wish to preteach the following vocabulary words: *prosperity, orphaned, orphanage, perplexed.*

Judith Gorog has been telling stories since she was a child. Born in Madison, Wisconsin, she was educated in California at the University of California in Berkeley and at Mills College in Oakland. Ms. Gorog now resides in Princeton, New Jersey, with her husband István and their three children, Antonia, Nicole, and Christopher.

Prosperity

by Judith Gorog

These sidenotes show how one reader thought about realistic and fantastic details while reading the story.

An <u>orphaned</u> boy stood by the side of a road, waiting. He had chosen a spot at the crest of a hill. From where he stood, concealed by tall weeds, he could see far down the road in both directions. Because of the hill, any approaching wagon would be going quite <u>slowly</u> by the time it reached him.

This sounds like a real boy doing real things, even though it's probably a long time ago. He's waiting for a ride on a wagon.

As the hours passed, the boy could hear, as well as feel, the <u>rumbling</u> of his empty stomach. Otherwise, the only sounds were the rasp of the insects and the rattle of the wind pushing dry seed pods one against the other.

The boy is hungry and now that it's dark, he's getting cold. This is still realistic.

No wagons came. The sun set; the evening breeze made the boy's skin prickle with cold. An hour after moonrise, he heard a wagon in the distance, then saw the lean old horse, milk-white in the moonlight, struggle up the hill.

Making Predictions: Have the students make predictions about what the boy is waiting for and why.

The boy crouched down in the weeds. He <u>recognized</u> neither horse nor wagon, but he'd need to see the driver first, before he dared to speak.

Response Clue: Students might point out some of the words with affixes that have been underlined.

At the crest of the hill, the wagon slowed, stopped. The driver, hunched on the wagon seat, turned his face toward the boy. He was very old, his face <u>ashen</u> in the moonlight. "Want a ride, boy? You running away?"

This sounds real, too. The old man has stopped to give the boy a ride.

"Only from the <u>orphanage</u>." The boy straightened up, taller than the weeds. "They don't really care." He took one step forward. "How'd you know I was here?"

ESL/LEP: Make sure students know the meaning of the idiom *running away*.

"Horse smelled you, and now we can both hear your stomach. Climb up. There's stew in the pot, still warm."

Could a horse really smell a boy hiding in a bush? I'm not sure if this is realistic or not. This part about both the man and horse hearing his stomach growl may be humor.

"Thank you, sir." The boy climbed into the wagon bed, and found the battered pot. <u>Sitting</u> crosslegged with the stewpot in his lap, he took his spoon from his pocket and ate, chewing every bite for a very long time. Who knew when he'd eat again?

Meanwhile, without a word from the old man, the horse <u>resumed</u> his slow pace. After a time, the boy stopped eating, not wanting to make the old man angry at him for being greedy. The boy felt almost satisfied, and hardly seemed to have made any difference in the level of stew in the pot, so probably he'd quit eating in time. The wagon creaked on through the deserted countryside, through moonshadow and moonlight. Carefully returning the stewpot to its place, the boy climbed up onto the wagon seat beside the old man, who mumbled something.

"Pardon, sir?" the boy asked.

"My turn," said the old man.

Perplexed by the old man's response, the boy was silent for a while, and then asked.

"Where you headed?"

"The town the foreigners made, the one they called 'Prosperity,'" the old man answered.

"'Prosperity?'" the boy repeated, a bit disappointed. He'd hoped to go somewhat farther away from the orphanage, even though they'd hardly look for him in Prosperity. No one went there, ever. "The ghost town?"

The old man nodded. "It's my turn."

"Turn to do what?" the boy ventured.

"When the foreigners dug a mine there, and built a railroad there, in the most sacred place in all the world, they made a great tear in the fabric of time. They disturbed the peace of many souls. I help to mend it."

"Help? How do you know what to do?"

"The spirits from the other side instruct us. My brother's service ends tonight. It is my turn." He gestured toward the wagon bed. "You sleep now. I'll awaken you when we arrive."

The boy wanted to hear more, and was not at all sure he wanted to sleep, not so sure he wanted to close his eyes while they approached souls not at peace, but the old man's tone left no room for argument, and the boy did feel all the accumulated tiredness of that whole, long day. Back he crawled, pulled on a scratchy wool blanket that smelled of horse, and was instantly asleep.

When he awoke, the moon was gone, the night dark and utterly silent. The horse had been unhitched from the wagon, and stood freshly groomed, pale and shimmering, as if from his own light.

The old man stood by the horse's head, stroking the animal and whispering.

The boy strained his ears to hear.

"My turn," the old man said.

Sitting up, the boy folded the blanket, stretched, and

◀ This pot of stew may be a fantastic detail. It was still warm, and after the boy had eaten, the pot seemed to have almost the same amount of stew.

Meeting Individual Needs: Have students read the sidenotes on pages 8 and 9, then ask them to underline the text that inspired these notes. Encourage them to write their own sidenote here about the realistic details in these paragraphs.

◀ The man says he's going to help mend a tear in the fabric of time. In real life, there's no such thing. This is a fantastic detail. The story must be a fantasy.

Now use the wide margins to write your own notes about the realistic and fantastic details in the story.
Response Clue: Ask students if this detail about the spirits sounds like something that could be in a realistic story or a fantasy. Have them explain their answers.

Response Clue: Ask students to tell if this detail about a horse that never tires seems to belong in a realistic story or a fantasy. Have them explain their answers.

Response Clue: Ask students what details about the stew and the stewpot make this story a fantasy.

climbed down from the wagon. Where would he go now? Into the ghost town that lay just beyond the forest? No. He'd walk back a mile or so to the crossroads, hope he'd find another ride, then a place where he could work.

"Here." The old man held out the reins toward the boy. Not <u>understanding</u>, the boy kept his hands at his sides. "Take them," the old man ordered. "Take the horse. He appears to be old to avoid exciting the envy of those who would steal him, but he never tires. Take the wagon and the stewpot. It is never empty. Go, and come back here to return them to me in seven years."

"Seven years?"

"Yes. In seven years." With that the old man <u>stepped</u> into the forest and was gone.

With a shudder, the boy hitched the horse to the wagon, climbed up and started off, back to the crossroads. Once there, he watered the horse at a nearby stream, and then <u>continued</u> on his way.

Seven years? The old man would most likely be dead in seven years, the horse for sure in less. Seven years? And the stewpot? Tying the reins loosely, the boy climbed back into the wagon, then <u>returned</u> to his seat with the stewpot in his arms. To his surprise, the stew was still warm, and tasted even better than before. One <u>spoonful</u> followed another into his mouth as the wagon rumbled slowly along. The boy filled his stomach until it hurt. The level of the stew in the pot did not change.

And so the seven years passed. The boy grew up, with horse and wagon to help him earn his way, and always enough to eat. He lived with a comfort and freedom he'd only <u>dreamed</u>.

At the end of the seven years, the horse, of his own accord, turned his head toward the ghost town called Prosperity. The boy had often debated with himself whether or not he'd return. He hadn't actually promised, after all. But the horse and the stewpot had served him well for seven years, until he was grown and strong. He could have let the horse go alone, but he didn't. He'd take them back and say his thank you.

It was long after the moon had set when the horse stopped beside the dark wood. The boy <u>unharnessed</u> the horse, rubbed him till his coat <u>glittered</u> in the night with a light all its own.

<u>Abruptly</u> the old man stood there beside him, looking not one minute older than when they had parted. Before the boy could speak, the old man clasped him <u>firmly</u> by the shoulders, turned him toward the forest that led to Prosperity, and in a tone that left no room for argument, said, "Your turn."

Summarizing: Have students stop at this point in the story and summarize what has happened so far.

Clarification: You may wish to have students reread this paragraph to clarify that the horse took the lead in returning to meet the man. The boy had often been uncertain about whether he would go back.

Additional Skills: This selection is also appropriate for teaching plot development (see ATE page 23).

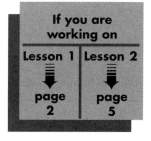

If you are working on

Lesson 1	Lesson 2
⬇	⬇
page 2	page 5

Preteaching Vocabulary: You may wish to preteach the following words: *cavernous, incense, airshaft, hypnotically, trance, bewildered, impertinent.*

Making Predictions: Have students skim the title and the first three paragraphs. Ask them to predict what will happen to the story character inside "the cave."

Use the wide margins to write your own thoughts about the realistic and fantastic details in this story.

Response Clue: Students might point out some of the words with affixes that have been underlined.

Response Clue: Ask students what hint they see in this paragraph that this story might be a fantasy. Suggest that they write their first sidenote about fantastic details here.

Response Clue: The older brother thinks the crocodiles look at him. This could be a fantastic detail.

ESL/LEP: Ask students to find and define the words with *-ed* suffixes in this paragraph. Reinforce that this suffix shows past tense.

Response Clue: Ask students if the story detail about the wooden horse seems to fit in a realistic story or a fantasy and have them explain their reasoning.

Enrique Jaramillo Levi (1944-   ) is a writer and poet who lives in Panama. The fantastic elements in his writing are part of a long tradition of this kind of literature by writers from Central and South America. Levi has also edited a collection of stories by Latin American women, *When New Flowers Bloom.*

The Cave

by Enrique Jaramillo Levi

A white dog with dark spots was sniffing around a fire hydrant in front of the store window. On the other side of the window, the shapes of objects looked blurred. I opened the door to my father's store and a little bell rang. When I was about to enter, I had the distinct impression that a large, cavernous mouth was going to swallow me. I went inside anyway.

I was welcomed by my cat. My sweet cat. His sad, crossed eyes looked at me tamely as he arched his back. Yellow, blue, and white neon lights flickered on and off. The walls had the familiar scents of incense and pine. I hesitated for a moment. I looked behind the counter and saw that my father was busy helping a client who looked Chinese. I continued walking toward that place I had been told many times not to enter.

After walking down the long hallway lined with old chests and forgotten furniture, I entered "the cave." That was what my older brother called it. He would tell me, "Dad stores all kinds of strange things in there. Every time I go inside, it seems that the stuffed crocodiles look at me as if they're unhappy. I wonder why those crocodiles are in the cellar. They're probably just iguanas or gigantic lizards Dad's collected."

All kinds of old clothing that looked like theater costumes hung on hooks randomly nailed into the walls of the cellar. I touched the silk, worn and dirty, and a horrible spider almost bit me. I screamed once and just then the little white wooden horse with the broken leg, which had disappeared mysteriously a long time ago, rocked forward, greeting me happily from his corner covered with cobwebs. The mild breeze that filtered through the airshaft gently swayed a piece of salted codfish that hung from the ceiling on a wire. I don't know what made me stretch out my hand at that moment and pull off a piece of that dark, leathery skin and chew on it, tasting the salt that reminded me of seas sailed by pirates.

I continued walking into the <u>darkness</u>. I sensed shadows moving in the back of the room and heard small, <u>squeaky</u> sounds. I started fighting the fear I was feeling and my heart started pounding like crazy. I felt strange <u>sensations</u> on my skin and I didn't know if it was just my imagination or if they were caused by spirits I couldn't see. I stopped to listen. Yes, now it was loud. I heard a screech. I lifted my foot; it became completely silent in the cave.

Twisted wires hanging out of boxes created strange shapes. Foul smells seeped from ancient bottles and made me feel dizzy. I suddenly saw the beady eyes of a huge rat. I screamed and saw them fade in the darkness. I felt strange things bumping into my ankles, and I took a step back. And another. I tripped on some rolled-up wire that I thought was a rattlesnake coiling around my feet. I wanted to run, but I tripped and fell into a box that was inside another larger box. I felt very small. And in fact I was, because I saw the enormous eyes of my cat shining like streetlights in the darkness. They stared at me for a long time, <u>hypnotically</u>, as if everything had suddenly stopped forever. The cat stretched out his big front paws and placed them on the edge of the larger box, breaking that strange trance we were in. As he was stretching, he lowered that gigantic, threatening head. I saw myself reflected in those liquid pools that continued staring at me. "It's me. . . Anita!" I said, trying to calm him down. But he opened his mouth wide. I was disgusted by the smell of codfish on his breath.

I saw the sharp points of his fangs coming closer. I could see them slowly penetrating the darkness. In one swift movement, I managed to grab onto one of the long, elastic hairs of his whiskers and swing on it with the hope of being able to jump out of the box. I closed my eyes so I wouldn't tremble before those bewildered crossed eyes that were right in front of me, that continued watching me sway from side to side.

I let go of his whisker and fell on the rolled-up wire, which wrapped itself around me. I couldn't move. I was a tiny doll trapped in a whirlpool of <u>metallic</u> waves that vibrated like shiny, new springs. A loud meow made me look up. His wide, dark mouth with sharp fangs was getting closer.

Suddenly a light was turned on. The cat ran away. My father's strong hands started to unravel the wires that had me trapped. I looked up at his face for some kind of an explanation, a signal. I saw only his usual expression, as

Additional Skills: This selection is also appropriate for teaching cause and effect (see ATE page 59).

Response Clue: Students might relate a similar experience when someone dismissed as a dream something that seemed very real.

if nothing out of the ordinary had happened. He helped me stand up and I brushed off the dust trying to get rid of the bad memories. Everything went back to normal. I confirmed this when the mirror on the wall reflected my normal height. But my bones ached. They felt strange, taut, and hot inside. A little bell rang. I knew a new customer was coming in. Dad left and made a gesture with his hand for me to follow him. Before leaving, I wanted to look at myself in the mirror one more time. I saw the cat approach me from behind. As usual, I was at least three times as big as he. Then the cat meowed. I turned around to face him. His crossed eyes shone under the light that hung from the ceiling. "You're not a bad kitten. . . are you?" I whispered. I felt the heat tingling in my bones. As my cat walked away, swaying his impertinent tail, I'm sure I saw him wink at me.

For weeks after, I felt a lot of pain in my bones when it rained, especially at night. I never again went near cats. My brother thinks that I fell asleep in the cave that day and had a bad nightmare. Of course that is the most logical explanation. Anybody would say that.

If you are working on

Lesson 1	Lesson 2
⬇	⬇
page 15	page 17

Reviewing *Recognizing Fantasy*

A. Read the short story "The Cave" on pages 12-14. As you read, use the wide margins to make notes about the realistic and fantastic details you find. Then use the chart below to analyze your observations.

Reviewing the Strategy: Have students refer to the sidenotes they wrote on pages 12-14. These notes will help them complete the chart. They should then decide if the story is a realistic one or a fantasy.

Question	Yes	No	Look back at details	Confirm
Are some of the places unlike places in the real world?	✓		The store looks like a giant mouth. "The cave" is filled with unusual items.	**Fantasy** or **Realistic Story?**
Do unusual events occur?	✓		A wooden horse seems to come alive. The girl becomes very small. The cat threatens the girl.	
Do some characters have traits or abilities that real people don't have?	✓		The girl can feel changes in her bones. The cat seems to wink at the girl.	

B. Do you think the narrator believes this was a nightmare? Why? What do you think happened?

Students may respond that they do believe it was a nightmare. Be sure they give

reasons that support their response. For example: people don't shrink in real life,

house cats are not larger than young girls, wire cannot wrap itself around a person.

Students may agree also with the brother, that she had a nightmare.

Managing the Lesson: Answers in the checklist are suggestions. Students may find additional details.

Cooperative Learning: Have the students complete Section B independently. Then ask groups to debate whether or not the narrator believes the action in the story is really a nightmare. Remind the students to refer to their sidenotes on pages 12-14.

Testing Recognizing Fantasy

Test-Taking Hints:
Tell students that when they take reading tests, they will have to think carefully about both choices before selecting one. Remind them to think about the strategy they have learned for deciding whether a story is a realistic one or a fantasy.

A. Read each excerpt below and decide whether it is part of a realistic story or a fantasy. Put an X in the box showing your choice. Then explain your answer on the line below it.

1. "He raised his fingers to his lips and whistled. 'Listen,' he shouted. 'Listen!' The men stood still. A minute passed, and then another—only the waves lapping on the beach could be heard in the terrifying stillness of the island."

from *The Black Stallion*, by Walter Farley

[X] realistic story   [] fantasy
Nothing happens in the excerpt that could not happen in real life.

Meeting Individual Needs: Students who find Section A challenging may need to look back at the charts on the **Introducing** and **Reviewing** pages.

2. "The tiger, checking himself in mid-leap just before he entered the shadow of the trees, caught fire in the air, became a tongue of flame lashing out at the dry black branches. . . ."

from *The Rule of Names*, by Ursula K. LeGuin

[] realistic story   [X] fantasy
A tiger could not change into a flame in real life.

3. ". . . she soon made out that she was in the pool of tears which she had wept when she was nine feet high. 'I wish I hadn't cried so much!' said Alice, as she swam about, trying to find her way out. 'I shall be punished for it now, I suppose, by being drowned in my own tears!'"

from *Alice in Wonderland* by Lewis Carroll

[] realistic story   [X] fantasy
In real life, people don't quickly change size.

Assessing Student Writing: Rate student writing on a scale of 1-4, with 1 being the least degree and 4 being the greatest degree. Use the following criteria: distinguishes between fantastic and realistic details, creates well-drawn characters and settings, displays original thought.

B. Write a short realistic description of something you did recently. Then rewrite the description so that it becomes fantasy.

Suggest that students change their realistic stories into fantasies by underlining some

of the realistic details, then substituting fantastic ones. You might want to encourage

them to exaggerate realistic characteristics of their characters, events, or setting.

_____

_____

_____

_____

_____

To begin Lesson 2

page 5

Reviewing *Base Words and Affixes*

A. Reread "The Cave" on pages 12-14. As you read, underline words that have bases and prefixes or suffixes. Choose one of the words you have found and analyze it in the diagram below.

Reviewing the Strategy: Show students how to follow the arrows on the diagram, moving from the word to its prefix and/or suffix and base word, and finally, to its meaning.

Managing the Lesson: Answers on the diagram are suggestions. Students may cite additional words, such as *cavernous* and *metallic*.

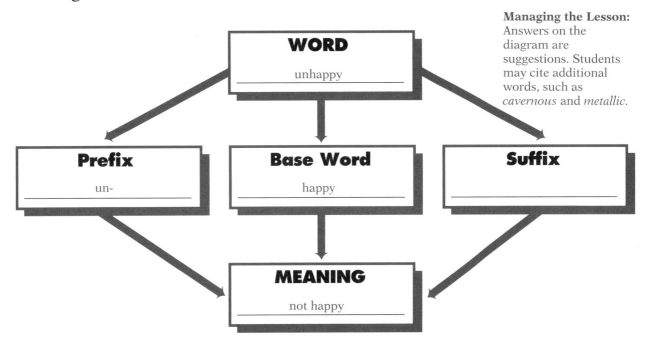

WORD
unhappy

Prefix
un-

Base Word
happy

Suffix

MEANING
not happy

B. Choose one of the base words below or select another base word you know. See how many interesting words you can create by adding prefixes and suffixes to it. Try adding both a prefix and a suffix to the same base word.

Individualized Learning: Have students complete the page independently. You may want to suggest that they use a dictionary for ideas.

night   treat   open

Students might suggest: nightly, midnight, treatment, treaty, reopen, unopened.

Test-Taking Hints: Remind students to carefully fill in the bubble next to the answer they choose. As they complete this test, have students keep in mind the strategy they learned for finding the base word and suffix or prefix of an unfamiliar word.

Testing Base Words and Affixes

A. Fill in the bubble next to the word or words with the same meaning as the boldfaced word below. Then write the base word and its affix and explain your choice on the line that follows.

1. Later I was told that I was talking **nonsense**.

- ❍ loudly
- ● without sense
- ❍ good sense
- ❍ bravely

base word: *sense*; prefix: *non-*; *nonsense* means "without sense"

2. When the priest came, Father asked me to **retell** my story.

- ❍ sing
- ● tell again
- ❍ go back to
- ❍ run

base word: *tell*; prefix: *re-*; *retell* means "to tell again"

3. As usual, my brother was **misleading** me.

- ❍ informing
- ● giving me bad advice
- ❍ teasing me
- ❍ taking me for granted

base word: *lead*; prefix: *mis-*; suffix: *-ing*; *misleading* means "giving bad or wrong advice"

4. The chef was feeling **uncreative**.

- ● not imaginative
- ❍ surprised
- ❍ not safe
- ❍ inspired

base word: *create*; prefix: *un-*; suffix: *-ive*; *uncreative* means "not imaginative"

5. The young woman was the first to **circumnavigate** the island.

- ❍ hike around
- ❍ swim to
- ❍ find on a globe
- ● sail around

base word: *navigate*; prefix: *circum-*; *circumnavigate* means "to sail around"

Assessing Student Writing: Rate student writing on a scale of 1-4, with 1 being the least degree and 4 being the greatest degree. Use the following criteria: uses affixes correctly, uses descriptive language, describes the scene clearly.

B. Write some sentences about a scary place you have visited. In your description, use at least five words that have affixes.

If students do not want to write about a real place, they may imagine one. Have them underline the base words and circle the affixes they use.

Unit *TWO*

BECOMING AN ACTIVE READER

Active readers are thinking readers. They form pictures in their mind of the setting and characters in the **short story**. Then they predict what might happen next. Finally, they check to see whether or not their predictions are correct.

Using Skills and Strategies

Reading between the lines, or **making inferences**, can help you understand even a puzzling story. You may ask: What just happened? Why did it happen? What do I know that helps me understand this? What is really going on?

Authors build your interest by creating problems their characters must face. This is often the conflict of the story. The **plot** of the story often tells how the characters solve this conflict. You may ask: What is the biggest problem that the characters face? How do the characters try to solve this problem? Which solutions don't work? Which solutions do work? What is the resolution of the conflict?

In this unit, learning to **make inferences** and identify parts of the **plot** will help you read stories actively.

The Short Story: The Writer's Voice

How do short story writers make us want to enter their imaginary worlds? Often they present characters who face problems similar to our own. We are caught up in the characters' conflicts, but we can learn from them, too. We can use what they learn to help us solve our own problems.

Responding to Short Stories

Good readers often compare characters' experiences with their own. As you read "Mr. Hollywood" and "The Scholarship Jacket," make notes in the margins about the comparisons you make between the characters' lives and your own life. Writing notes will help you remember your responses. Use these notes as you discuss the stories with your classmates.

Unit Enrichment: Students may enjoy acting out the stories in this unit. You might even challenge them to write their own story to act out. Some students may write a new story or a "screenplay" for one of these stories, some may act, some may direct, and some may perform the behind-the-scene duties. Encourage them to plan and rehearse, then put on their performance for the rest of the school or take it "on-the-road" to a convalescent or retirement home in the community.

Making Inferences

Lesson 3	Introducing *page 20*	Practicing *page 21*	Applying *page 22*	Reviewing *page 34*	Testing *page 35*

Lesson Objective: To combine story information with prior knowledge to make inferences in the short stories "Mr. Hollywood" and "The Scholarship Jacket."

Oral Language: Discuss the meaning and use of the expression *reading between the lines*. Ask students to model this in conversation.

Modeling the Strategy: Read aloud a passage from students' classroom text to model making inferences. Refer to the steps in the diagram. After completing the page, use the Reproducible Activity Master on page T12 of the ATE to help students apply this strategy to "Mr. Hollywood."

Managing the Lesson: Remind students to use the sidenotes on pages 26-27 to model the process of active reading and to help them answer questions 1 and 2.

Introducing Strategies

The process of **making inferences** is sometimes called "reading between the lines." Good readers make inferences by combining information in the selection with what they already know. Study the diagram below, which shows how you can make inferences in your reading and in your life.

Reading the Short Story

Read "Mr. Hollywood" on pages 26-29 and the sidenotes on pages 26-27. These notes show how one reader made inferences about the story. Use these sidenotes to help you complete the items below.

1. Select two inferences the reader made in the sidenotes. What story details did the reader use to make these inferences?

Student may suggest: Because J.W. feels left out, he is late to class several times;

because J.W. feels left out, he thinks the other students are nerdy.

_____

_____

2. How did the reader combine personal experiences or knowledge with this evidence to make inferences?

Students may suggest: The reader has felt left out in a new situation and thinks J.W.

might, too; the reader assumes J.W. is shy because he or she knows that people

sometimes cover up shyness with an aggressive attitude.

Practicing Making Inferences

A. Read each passage, then circle the letter of the correct statement. More than one statement in each item may be correct. Explain your answer on the lines below.

1. The classroom was set up in small groups again, and everyone was busy, laughing and talking.

    (a.) The students all know each other.

    b. The class is waiting for the teacher to tell them what to do.

    c. It is the first day of a new school year.

    (d.) The students are comfortable working together.

Students should mention that the students' laughing and working together indicate

they know each other and are comfortable working together.

2. "And, my dear," he pretended to tell her [Mrs. Morris], "what goes on *behind* the scenes is as important as what goes on *in* the scenes!"

    a. At this point in the story, J.W. likes Mrs. Morris a lot.

    b. J.W. likes telling secrets.

    c. J.W. is interested in acting on stage.

    (d.) J.W. knows about what makes a play or show run smoothly.

Students answers should mention that J.W. has had behind-the-scenes experience at

another school and that he probably feels he could help in his new school.

B. When J.W. is feeling lonely, scared, and left out, he writes a rap. If he were to come to you for advice, how might you help him feel more at home?

Students might suggest that J.W. should be more friendly to Tanesha and maybe

show her his rap or that he should find someone who lives near him to help him with

his bus route. Students' advice will reflect story details and their own experiences with

being in a new situation.

_____

_____

_____

_____

_____

_____

Purpose: The purpose of this page is to help students practice making inferences in a short story. Questions reflect the strategy of combining story details with prior knowledge illustrated in the diagram on the **Introducing** page.

Peer Sharing: Have students complete Section A independently, then work with a partner to compare answers. Encourage students to discuss which story details and personal experiences helped them make these inferences.

Conferencing: Have students work with a peer to circle the story details and personal experiences in each others' writing.

Applying the Skill to Other Disciplines: Have students write sidenotes on notebook paper to illustrate how they make inferences as they read science, social studies, or other assignments.

ESL/LEP: Use props and gestures to introduce baseball terms such as *inning, out, pitch, batter,* and *scoreboard* before students read the excerpt.

Individualized Learning: Have students complete the page independently. Make sure that their explanations cite story details and prior experience when they make their inferences.

Applying Making Inferences

A. Read the following story excerpt and answer the questions that follow it. In this story, a father is sitting in the stands at a baseball game watching his son pitch. It is now the last half of the ninth inning, and the first batter has just been called out. So far, the son has pitched a perfect game—that is, no player has even gotten on base.

> *The red eye on the scoreboard showed the first out.*
> *"Nearly there, nearly there," crooned the woman.*
> *The . . . man put an arm around his [the father's] shoulder, and the gap-toothed man was cheekily patting him on the back. The owner of the radio had turned it up full volume to celebrate.*
> *"Don't congratulate me yet," he begged them, shrugging them off. But what he really felt like saying was yes, congratulate me, hug me all of you, let's laugh and enjoy ourselves.*
>
> from *"The Perfect Game" by Sergio Ramirez*

1. Who are the woman, the man, and the gap-toothed man? How were you able to infer this?

All three are spectators sitting near the boy's father in the stands. They are sitting

close enough to talk to him and touch him.

2. Explain why the father both does and does not want the others to congratulate him.

He is excited and he wants to celebrate, but he is cautious because the game

isn't over yet.

Writing Process: Students might choose to develop their descriptive paragraph into the first draft of a poem or short story.

B. Write a paragraph in which you describe what the father is thinking as he watches the game. Use story evidence and what you already know to make your inferences.

Students might suggest: The father is excited and proud of his child's abilities and

accomplishments. He hopes the game will be over soon so he can celebrate and so

nothing can happen to spoil the game.

To review
↓
page 34

Plot

Lesson 4 | **Introducing** page 23 | **Practicing** page 24 | **Applying** page 25 | **Reviewing** page 36 | **Testing** page 37

Introducing Strategies

The **plot** of the story is the series of events that builds suspense. The process that sets this series in motion is the **conflict** of the story. The attempts to solve the conflict are presented in the **rising action**, which leads to the high point, or **climax**, of the story. This is when the action is strongest or the problem is at its worst. The climax is followed by the **resolution,** when the conflict ends and the outcome of the action becomes clear. The remaining problems are presented in the **falling action**.

The chart below shows a strategy you can use to keep track of events that develop the plot in a story.

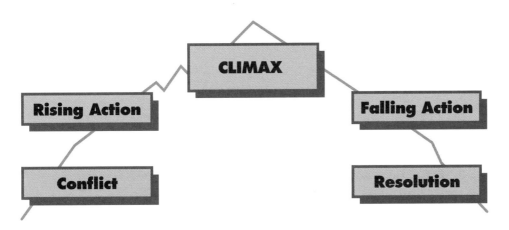

Reading the Short Story

Reread "Mr. Hollywood" on pages 26-29. As you read, keep track of the plot by circling the events as they occur. Use this information to answer the questions below.

1. What is the conflict of the story? How does J.W. react to this conflict?

The conflict is that J.W. is new in school and hasn't figured out a way to fit in. He

reacts by keeping to himself.

2. How does J.W.'s reaction lead to the story's climax?

The students don't know J.W. can help because he has been so quiet. He finally jumps

in to organize the rehearsal.

Lesson Objective: To recognize plot by identifying conflict, rising action, climax, falling action, and resolution in stories.

ESL/LEP: Have students discuss an episode of a TV show they have seen. Ask them to describe the action, conflicts between characters, and the high point of the story.

Modeling the Strategy: Read aloud a passage from students' classroom texts to model identifying the plot of a short story. Refer to the steps in the diagram. After completing the page, use the Reproducible Activity Master on page T11 of the ATE to help students apply the strategy to "Mr. Hollywood."

Managing the Lesson: Remind students that they can use the events they circled in the story to help them answer questions 1 and 2.

Practicing Plot

A. Circle the letter of the item that best completes each statement. Then, on the line that follows, explain your choice.

1. The conflict of the story is whether or not
   a. J.W. will be put on detention for being late.
   b. the students will accept and respect J.W.
   c. J.W. get his classwork done on time.
   d. J.W. will find a way to fit in at his new school.

   If he had fit in, J.W. might have taken charge of the rehearsal from the beginning.

2. The climax of the story occurs when J.W.
   a. is late for school.
   b. gets the opportunity to help out during rehearsal for the talent show.
   c. writes a rap.
   d. eats lunch by himself in the cafeteria.

   J.W. overcomes his shyness and organizes the students.

3. The conflict is resolved when
   a. J.W. finishes his assignment quickly.
   b. Mrs. Morris loses her reputation as a good teacher.
   c. J.W. gets the opportunity to show that he can help by directing the talent show.
   d. Tanesha asks to hear J.W.'s rap.

   J.W. suddenly feels that he has found a place where he is needed.

B. How does understanding the story's climax help you understand its plot? Use story details to explain your answer.

Student answers will vary, but should reflect understanding that the climax leads to

the resolution. Students may suggest that once you see J.W. in action, organizing the

rehearsal, you understand just how smart and talented he is. At first you just know he

is frustrated and lonely. When he bursts into action and everyone follows his direction

without question, you realize that he will fit into his new school.

Purpose: The purpose of this page is to help students practice identifying plot in the short story. Questions reflect the strategy illustrated in the diagram on the **Introducing** page.

Peer Sharing: Have students complete Section A with a classmate. Encourage them to refer to the events they circled in the story as they discuss their answers.

Cooperative Learning: Have students complete Section B in groups of three. Encourage them to work together to develop their responses.

Assessing Cooperative Work: As you observe groups, note the degree to which members listen to each other, contribute to the discussion, and add relevant information. Then have each group member rate himself or herself on these criteria.

Applying *Plot*

A. Read the excerpt below, paying special attention to the events as they happen. Then answer the questions that follow.

> *As I recall, it all began at the end of September. My birthday was about to arrive, and my mother was making me a new shirt. As she sat working on it, her face turned pale and she began to cough. Her eyes grew wide and she stood up. . . . Then she walked into the other room.*
>
> from "As I Am . . . As I Was" by Lino Novas-Calvo

1. Do the events described take place before or after the narrator's birthday? How do you know?

Before. The story says Lino's birthday was about to arrive.

2. What is the first sign that something is wrong with the mother?

Lino's mother's face turns pale and she begins to cough.

3. What conflict is building in the story?

The mother is beginning to look ill.

4. How do you think the story will end?

Students might suggest that it sounds as if she will become ill and die.

B. Briefly describe the plot of a book you have read or of a movie or TV show. Jot down the important events in the story, identify the climax, and tell how the story ends.

Students should describe a plot of a book, movie, or TV show by listing events in the

story and identifying the elements of plot, including the story's climax and resolution.

Applying the Skill to Other Media: Students might enjoy describing the action of a movie to help them identify the elements of its plot.

ESL/LEP: To introduce the terms *before* and *after*, show students a picture of items or people in a line. Then use gestures to identify items or individuals that are before and after others in the line.

Individualized Learning: Have students complete the page independently. Make sure that their explanations for Section A display an understanding of plot.

Assessing Student Writing: Rate student writing on a scale of 1-4, with 1 being the least degree and 4 being the greatest degree. Use the following criteria: uses logical order, includes details, resolves story conflict.

To review
page 36

Preteaching Vocabulary: You may wish to preteach the following vocabulary words: *evidence, advice, crooned, cheekily, attempts, detention, reputation.*

Jerdine Nolen Harold is a writer and middle-school educator who lives in Baltimore, Maryland. As a teacher, she especially enjoys helping her students think creatively and solve problems. Her skills in these areas are revealed in this short story.

Mr. Hollywood

by Jerdine Nolen Harold

The notes in the margin show how one reader made inferences about the story.

He's late, and everybody else is already working. He must feel left out; I know I would.

Making Predictions: You may wish to ask students to make predictions on what the selection is about after they read its title and headnote.

He's new in school, and he has an attitude. He calls the bus connections "stupid," and he kicks the desk. I know someone who covers up shyness this way.

He really doesn't know for sure that these kids are nerdy; he doesn't even know them. I used to have a friend who would say mean things because she was afraid people were saying mean things about *her*.

I was right. He's scared and shy and is covering it up. I'd feel the same way. The other kids have had almost a whole year to get to know each other.

Response Clue: Ask students to guess the story's conflict. Note the plot points circled.

I wonder what he means— "behind the scenes."

It didn't matter that the boy walked into his English class late again. For him, it was going to be another "do nothing kind of day." He put the late pass on the teacher's desk and made his way around the maze of bookbags, desks, and clusters of kids. The classroom was set up in small groups again, and everyone was busy, laughing and talking. The room sounded like a hive of hungry bees. And the honey seemed oh, so sweet. They were getting ready for the "All School Talent Show."

"Good morning, Julius," the teacher said as he passed her.

"Mrs. Morris, could you please call me J.W.? And I'm late because it's hard to make those stupid bus connections in a new neighborhood," he said, kicking a desk.

"*Try*. You know, if you had gotten here on time today you could have joined Joe's group. They had to make some changes and could have used extra help."

Joe Brown looked over at J.W. and tried to catch his eye. But J.W. avoided him. He managed a weak smile at Joe as he looked at the nerdy types Joe had to work with. He was glad he was not in that group. And it was no skin off his nose if Joe was stuck! Besides, he didn't have to beg anyone to let him join a group. He was his own group. You'd think they'd give him a little slack after he had to transfer into the school so late in the year. And his dad had said this would be easy for him. (Riiiiight!) No matter—school would be over in a couple of weeks anyway.

J.W. moved a desk near the window. He turned his back to the class. He had to do an assignment Mrs. Morris had given him, to get him "caught up." (Riiiiight!) He knew she wasn't going to collect it anyway. She had her hands full with the talent show. And from where he sat, and with all due respect, she didn't know what she was doing. For example, she didn't even have anyone signed up for the behind-the-scenes stuff!

"And, my dear," he pretended to tell her, "what goes on *behind* the scenes is as important as what goes on *in* the scenes!"

He had done shows like these back at Carver Middle School. That's how he earned the name "Mr. Hollywood." He had gotten so good at organizing, producing, and directing that he could do it anywhere, including here at Hardwood Middle. But no one here knew of his reputation. And he certainly wasn't telling. Besides, no one *really* seemed interested in him. He wasn't about to audition his talents for the uninterested.

J.W. sat looking out the window with his notebook on his lap. The assignment wouldn't take half his brain. So he got it out of the way quickly. Then he made pictures out of the leaves on the trees the way some people use clouds. Doing that made him want to write a rap. He had started to write when the bell rang. It was time for lunch. He would finish it then. He needed something to do to pass the time, anyway.

In the cafeteria J.W. dodged the same groups of bodies from English class. The entire school was involved in the talent show. It hadn't been like that at Carver. Here at Hardwood, *everybody* was in the production, talent or no talent. Everybody but him.

He sat at his corner lunch table hunched over his notepad. He didn't feel hungry when the creative juices were flowing. (This was going to be a dynamite rap!) He was so involved with his rap that he didn't notice the crowd forming near his table.

"Hi, excuse me," someone said. He looked up. It was Tanesha Herbert. She sat at his table in Tech Ed.

"I'm . . ."

"Tanesha Herbert," he completed the introduction for her.

"Hi, you're new. You're in my Tech Ed class, right?"

"Yes, three days new. We sit at the same table."

"Well, I need to borrow this chair. May I?"

"Sure, it's not my chair," J.W. teased. They laughed at his attempted joke.

"By the way, I'm . . ." he began.

"Julius White," now it was her turn to finish.

"Uh, J.W. My friends call me J.W.," he said, cringing. They both noticed his embarrassment and giggled.

"What are you writing? A letter to a girlfriend back at your old school?"

"No, a rap!"

"For the talent show?"

Making Predictions: Ask students to use story information and what they already know to predict how the conflict might be resolved.

◀ So that's it. I bet he's feeling too shy to say what he's good at.

Response Clue: Students might note a time when they felt left out.

◀ I was right.

◀ He must be pretty smart; he does his assignment easily and quickly.

◀ To call the kids "groups of bodies" makes it seem like he doesn't want to know them. I think he's lonely and won't admit it.

◀ He's good at a lot of things. J.W. probably isn't as snobby as he sounds. I know people who act stuck up but who are really just feeling left out.

As you read, continue writing your own notes in the margins about inferences you make.

Additional Skills: This selection is also appropriate for teaching sequence (see ATE page 56) and cause and effect (see ATE page 59).

ESL/LEP: Define the idiom *price I have to pay* for the students.

Response Clue: Encourage students to use the information in the story and what they know to make inferences about whether or not J.W. might come to fit in at his new school.

Response Clue: Students may infer that something bad is going to happen soon. You might suggest that they write a sidenote here.

ESL/LEP: Define the idiom *to make waves* for the students.

"No, just for me. I'm not doing anything for the talent show. That's one price I have to pay for transferring so late in the school year. Besides, it would be like the work wasn't mine."

"You sound *seriously* creative."

"Well, you know how it is!"

"You'd be more than welcome in our talent show group. We're a bit unorganized, but . . ."

"No, thanks. I'm pretty busy just getting caught up with schoolwork."

"Could I hear your rap?"

"Maybe sometime, sure," he smiled at the attention.

Tanesha waved good-bye. She heard her friends calling her. J.W. watched her leave. Then the people at her table looked at him and waved. Against his better judgment, he waved back. Two girls whispered something to Tanesha and giggled.

He looked at his rap again. Maybe he'd stop this one and start a new one. "Let's see," he thought, "what rhymes with *Tanesha* . . ." he thought.

The next day Mrs. Morris's English class met in the auditorium. She handed him some papers as he gave her his late pass. It was the assignment she'd given him yesterday. There was a note attached:

Julius—A good paper, but where are YOUR THOUGHTS??? Redo questions 1-5 . . . and EXTEND yourself, please!

She handed him another packet of work. "Thought extenders," she said.

He looked at her, then at his feet. He sat down hard several rows away from her.

J.W. couldn't help breathing hard. He was mad. He couldn't believe it. He, "Mr. Hollywood," was sitting on the sidelines doing busy work with a rehearsal going on. He kept his head down, buried in his papers.

Mr. James, the school librarian, came in. He whispered something to Mrs. Morris. She walked quickly out of the room. Mr. James stood with his arms folded across his chest. J.W. looked up. Mr. James mustered an awkward smile in J.W.'s direction. J.W. tried not to notice. It was apparent that Mr. James knew less about putting on shows than Mrs. Morris did.

Some of the kids immediately saw the opportunity to get on the stage. Mr. James was the kind of person who didn't want to make waves. He would have let the entire school get up there if they asked. With that many people on stage, J.W. knew there would be trouble. Some of the kids were horsing around too close to the edge of the stage. A couple of kids were trying to touch the overhead lights while someone flicked them on and off. That curtain wouldn't last long either at the rate they were opening and closing it.

J.W. flew into action. He knew how dangerous this kind of thing could be. These kids had no self-control and no respect for the theater. J.W. went right into his "Mr. Hollywood" mode. He moved quickly because he knew he didn't have much of a leg to stand on. But the kids listened to his directions and followed them. In a matter of minutes, he had transformed the room from chaos to order.

Group by group came onto the stage to rehearse. J.W. directed them the whole time. He was in charge, "Mr. Hollywood." Because he was so natural at this, his commands were followed without question.

Joe Brown and his group got on the stage to do a spooky kind of rap. J.W. rushed to the light booth and flickered the lights. It gave the skit meaning on another level. The kids in Mrs. Morris's English class had never seen this kind of handiwork from another student. Some even cheered and applauded, Tanesha Herbert among them. Of course, it was no big deal for J.W. He was capable of doing this and much more.

When Mrs. Morris returned, she was surprised at the quiet. She was even more astonished to see J.W. waving his arms, directing her class, and organizing them. This seemingly uninterested student was moving people and props like he had done this kind of thing his whole life.

"I think I see some *extending* going on, Mr. Julius White!" Mrs. Morris smiled.

"Please, Mrs. Morris," J.W. beamed at the joke, "call me, 'Mr. Hollywood'!"

ESL/LEP: Define the idiom *horsing around* for the students.

ESL/LEP: Define the idiom *didn't have much of a leg to stand on* for the students.

Response Clue: Ask students to state how the conflict is resolved in their own words.

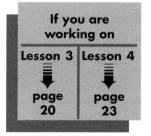

If you are working on

Lesson 3	Lesson 4
⬇	⬇
page 20	page 23

Preteaching Vocabulary:
You may wish to preteach
the following vocabulary
words: *embarrassing,
political, racist, resolution,
wealthy.*

Motivating Question: As
students read, ask them what
Salinas might be saying
about human nature.

**As you read, write your
own ideas about making
inferences. Use the wide
margins for your notes.**

Response Clue: Students
should circle key events to
help them keep track of the
plot. Note the examples
circled.

Response Clue: Tell
students to combine story
details with what they
already know to make an
inference about Martha's
character.

Response Clue: Have
students make an inference
about the importance of the
jacket to Martha. Suggest
that they write it in a
sidenote.

Response Clue: Ask
students to use story details
and their own experiences to
make inferences about how
Martha feels about herself.

Marta Salinas was born in Coalinga, California. She studied creative writing at the University of California, Irvine, and has written stories for the *Los Angeles Herald Examiner and California Living.* This story, which reflects her Mexican American heritage, is from a collection called *Nosotras: Latina Literature Today.*

The Scholarship Jacket

by Marta Salinas

The small Texas school that I attended carried out a tradition every year during the eighth grade graduation; a beautiful gold and green jacket, the school colors, was awarded to the class valedictorian, the student who had maintained the highest grades for eight years. The scholarship jacket had a big gold S on the left front side and the winner's name was written in gold letters on the pocket.

My oldest sister Rosie had won the jacket a few years back and I fully expected to win also. I was fourteen and in the eighth grade. I had been a straight A student since the first grade, and the last year I had looked forward to owning that jacket. My father was a farm laborer who couldn't earn enough money to feed eight children, so when I was six I was given to my grandparents to raise. We couldn't participate in sports at school because there were registration fees, uniform costs, and trips out of town; so even though we were quite agile and athletic, there would never be a sports school jacket for us. This one, the scholarship jacket, was our only chance.

In May, close to graduation, spring fever struck, and no one paid any attention in class; instead we stared out the windows and at each other, wanting to speed up the last few weeks of school. I despaired every time I looked in the mirror. Pencil thin, not a curve anywhere, I was called "Beanpole" and "String Bean" and I knew that's what I looked like. . . . [A] brain, that's what I had. That really isn't much for a fourteen-year-old to work with, I thought, as I absentmindedly wandered from my history class to the gym. Another hour of sweating in basketball and displaying my toothpick legs was coming up. Then I remembered my P.E. shorts were still in a bag under my desk where I'd forgotten them. I had to walk all the way back and get them. Coach Thompson was a real bear if anyone wasn't dressed for P.E. . . .

I was almost back at my classroom's door when I heard angry voices and arguing. I stopped. I didn't mean to eavesdrop; I just hesitated, not knowing what to do. I needed those shorts and I was going to be late, but I didn't want to interrupt an argument between my teachers. I recognized the voices: Mr. Schmidt, my history teacher, and Mr. Boone, my math teacher. They seemed to be arguing about me. I couldn't believe it. I still remember the shock that rooted me flat against the wall as if I were trying to blend in with the graffiti written there.

"I refuse to do it! I don't care who her father is, her grades don't even begin to compare to Martha's. I won't lie or falsify records. Martha has a straight A plus average and you know it." That was Mr. Schmidt and he sounded very angry. Mr. Boone's voice sounded calm and quiet.

"Look, Joann's father is not only on the Board, he owns the only store in town; we could say it was a close tie and—"

The pounding in my ears drowned out the rest of the words, only a word here and there filtered through. ". . . Martha is Mexican. . . . resign. . . . won't do it. . . ." Mr. Schmidt came rushing out, and luckily for me went down the opposite way toward the auditorium, so he didn't see me. Shaking, I waited a few minutes and then went in and grabbed my bag and fled from the room. Mr. Boone looked up when I came in but didn't say anything. . . .

The next day when the principal called me into his office, I knew what it would be about. He looked uncomfortable and unhappy. I decided I wasn't going to make it any easier for him so I looked him straight in the eye. He looked away and fidgeted with the papers on his desk.

"Martha," he said, "there's been a change in policy this year regarding the scholarship jacket. As you know, it has always been free." He cleared his throat and continued. "This year the Board decided to charge fifteen dollars—which still won't cover the complete cost of the jacket."

I stared at him in shock and a small sound of dismay escaped my throat. I hadn't expected this. He still avoided looking in my eyes.

"So if you are unable to pay the fifteen dollars for the jacket, it will be given to the next one in line."

Standing with all the dignity I could muster, I said, "I'll speak to my grandfather about it, sir, and let you know tomorrow." I cried on the walk home from the bus stop. The dirt road was a quarter of a mile from the

Making Predictions: Have students predict the outcome of the argument. Ask them to explain their predictions.

Response Clue: Help students identify the rising action circled in this paragraph.

ESL/LEP: Explain that the idiom *looked him straight in the eye* means "stared at him." Discuss the idea that in many cultures looking directly into a person's eyes is considered disrespectful.

Response Clue: Have students make inferences about why the principal told Martha she would have to pay for her jacket.

highway, so by the time I got home, my eyes were red and puffy.

. . . I knew I had to be honest with Grandpa; it was my only chance. He saw me and looked up.

He waited for me to speak. I cleared my throat nervously and clasped my hands behind my back so he wouldn't see them shaking. "Grandpa, I have a big favor to ask you," I said in Spanish, the only language he knew. He still waited silently. I tried again. "Grandpa, this year the principal said the scholarship jacket is not going to be free. It's going to cost fifteen dollars and I have to take the money in tomorrow, otherwise it'll be given to someone else." The last words came out in an eager rush. . . . I waited, desperately hoping he'd say I could have the money.

He turned to me and asked quietly, "What does a scholarship jacket mean?"

I answered quickly; maybe there was a chance. "It means you've earned it by having the highest grades for eight years and that's why they're giving it to you." Too late I realized the significance of my words. Grandpa knew that I understood it was not a matter of money. It wasn't that. He went back to hoeing the weeds that sprang up between the delicate little bean plants. . . .

"Then if you pay for it, Martha, it's not a scholarship jacket, is it? Tell your principal I will not pay the fifteen dollars."

I walked back to the house and locked myself in the bathroom for a long time. I was angry with grandfather even though I knew he was right, and I was angry with the Board, whoever they were. Why did they have to change the rules just when it was my turn to win the jacket?

It was a very sad and withdrawn girl who dragged into the principal's office the next day. This time he did look me in the eyes.

"What did your grandfather say?"

I sat very straight in my chair.

"He said to tell you he won't pay the fifteen dollars."

The principal muttered something I couldn't understand under his breath, and walked over to the window. He stood looking out at something outside. . . .

"Why?" he finally asked. "Your grandfather has the money. Doesn't he own a small bean farm?"

I looked at him, forcing my eyes to stay dry. "He said if I had to pay for it, then it wouldn't be a scholarship

ESL/LEP: Ask students why they think Martha uses her native language here.

Response Clue: Ask students to make inferences about why grandfather refused to pay the fifteen dollars.

Response Clue: Help students identify that this scene in the principal's office is the climax of the story.

jacket," I said and stood up to leave. "I guess you'll just have to give it to Joann." I hadn't meant to say that; it had just slipped out. I was almost to the door when he stopped me.

"Martha—wait. . . . We'll make an exception in your case. I'll tell the Board, you'll get your jacket."

I could hardly believe it. I spoke in a trembling rush. "Oh, thank you sir!" Suddenly I felt great. I didn't know about adrenalin in those days, but I knew something was pumping through me, making me feel as tall as the sky. I wanted to yell, jump, run the mile, do something. I ran out so I could cry in the hall where there was no one to see me. At the end of the day, Mr. Schmidt winked at me and said, "I hear you're getting a scholarship jacket this year."

His face looked as happy and innocent as a baby's, but I knew better. Without answering I gave him a quick hug and ran to the bus. I cried on the walk home again, but this time because I was so happy. I couldn't wait to tell Grandpa and ran straight to the field. I joined him in the row where he was working and without saying anything I crouched down and started pulling up the weeds with my hands. Grandpa worked alongside me for a few minutes, but he didn't ask what had happened. After I had a little pile of weeds between the rows, I stood up and faced him.

"The principal said he's making an exception for me, Grandpa, and I'm getting the jacket after all. That's after I told him what you said."

Grandpa didn't say anything, he just gave me a pat on the shoulder and a smile. He pulled out the crumpled red handkerchief that he always carried in his back pocket and wiped the sweat off his forehead.

"Better go see if your grandmother needs any help with supper."

I gave him a big grin. He didn't fool me. I skipped and ran back to the house whistling some silly tune.

Response Clue: Help students identify that these two paragraphs are part of the falling action.

Response Clue: Ask students to make inferences about what Mr. Schmidt wasn't saying.

Response Clue: At the resolution of the story, have students make inferences about what Martha meant when she said, "He didn't fool me."

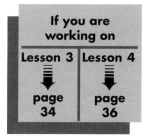

If you are working on

Lesson 3	Lesson 4
⬇	⬇
page 34	page 36

The Scholarship Jacket ■ **33**

Reviewing Making Inferences

A. Read the story "The Scholarship Jacket" on pages 30-33. As you read, make notes in the margins about how the information in the story and what you already know help you make inferences. On the chart below, describe how you made two of your inferences.

Managing the Lesson: Answers on the diagram are suggestions. Students may make additional inferences.

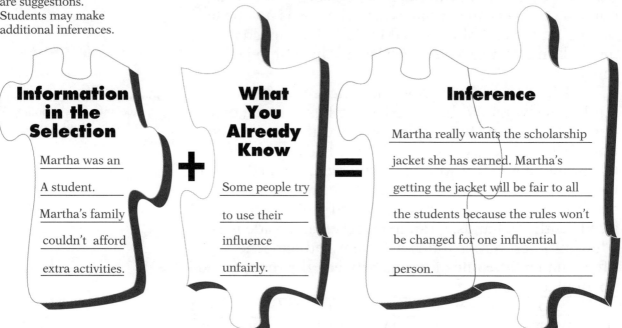

Information in the Selection

Martha was an A student. Martha's family couldn't afford extra activities.

+

What You Already Know

Some people try to use their influence unfairly.

=

Inference

Martha really wants the scholarship jacket she has earned. Martha's getting the jacket will be fair to all the students because the rules won't be changed for one influential person.

Peer Sharing: Have students complete Section A with a classmate. Partners should discuss how they made their inferences.

ESL/LEP: Allow students to include drawings in their character sketch of Grandfather.

Assessing Students Writing: Rate student writing on a scale of 1-4, with 1 being the least degree and 4 being the greatest degree. Use these criteria: understands Grandfather's character, uses story clues, makes valid inferences.

B. Write a brief character sketch of Grandfather. Be sure to tell which story clues you combined with what you already know to make your inferences.

Students may note that Grandfather refused to give Martha the money and that he

smiled but had to take out his handkerchief when she told him she was getting the

jacket after all. Students may write that they already know that it's hard to stand up

for what you believe in, but that when you do it anyway, things usually turn out well.

They may conclude that Grandfather is wise and sensitive.

_____

_____

_____

_____

_____

Testing Making Inferences

A. Fill in the circle next to each true statement. Then, on the line that follows it, explain your choice.

1. ● Martha thinks her P.E. class is both embarrassing and fun.
   ○ Martha hates P.E. more than just about anything.

   Students might suggest that she felt uncomfortable about her looks, but liked to be active.

2. ● Mr. Schmidt, Martha's history teacher, feels that efforts not to award Martha the jacket are unfair, political, and perhaps racist.
   ○ Mr. Boone, the math teacher, feels that Joann is smarter than Martha.

   Students may refer to Mr. Schmidt's protests about giving the award to Joann.

3. ○ Changing the rules about having to pay for the jacket was a way for the school to save money.
   ● Changing the rules about having to pay for the jacket is a plan designed to give the award to Joann.

   Students may refer to the conversation between Martha and the principal.

4. ○ At the end of the story, Grandpa is very disappointed in Martha.
   ● At the end of the story, Grandpa is proud of Martha.

   Students may refer to the grandfather's pat on Martha's shoulder and his smile.

B. Why do you think Martha's grandfather refused to pay for the jacket? Use story information and what you already know to make your inferences.

Students may point out that Grandfather asked why the jacket was called a

scholarship jacket if students had to pay for it. He knew that Martha's older sister

hadn't had to pay for hers and didn't want to give in to unfairness. Students may say

they have had experience with asking adults for money and with being treated

unfairly. They may conclude that Grandfather refuses to pay because he believes the

school is treating Martha unfairly and does not want to act dishonorably.

_____

_____

_____

_____

Test-Taking Hints: Remind students to read both answer choices carefully before they make their selection.

Meeting Individual Needs: Clarify that what people do can say more about their character than what they say. If necessary, read the directions and answer choices aloud.

Student Self-Assessment: Students might wish to evaluate their own writing on a scale of 1-4, with 1 being the least degree and 4 being the greatest degree. Have them use the following criteria: Did I answer the question? Did I use story information in my answer? Did I use what I already know? Did I make logical inferences?

To begin Lesson 4 page 23

Reviewing the Strategy: Have students refer to their sidenotes on pages 30-33 to complete the diagram. Tell students to use these notes to complete the chart.

Managing the Lesson: Answers on the diagram are suggestions. Students may cite additional details.

Reviewing Plot

A. Reread "The Scholarship Jacket" on pages 30-33, paying special attention to how the plot develops. Circle the main events, or rising action, and underline the story's climax and resolution. Draw double lines below the falling action. Then, use this information to complete the diagram below.

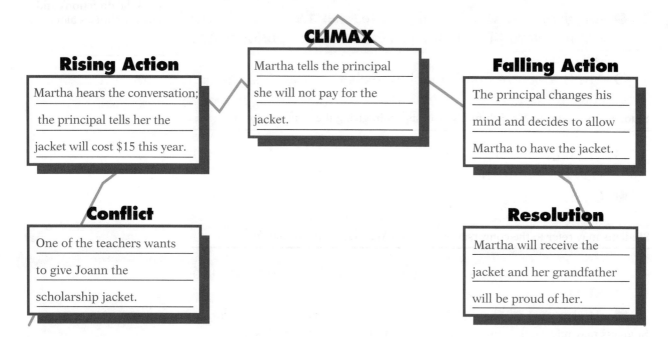

CLIMAX

Martha tells the principal she will not pay for the jacket.

Rising Action

Martha hears the conversation; the principal tells her the jacket will cost $15 this year.

Falling Action

The principal changes his mind and decides to allow Martha to have the jacket.

Conflict

One of the teachers wants to give Joann the scholarship jacket.

Resolution

Martha will receive the jacket and her grandfather will be proud of her.

Cooperative Learning: Have students complete Section A in groups of three. One student should read, another moderate, and the third record their findings. Tell students there should be a consensus on their responses.

Student Self-Assessment: Students might wish to evaluate their own writing on a scale of 1-4, with 1 being the least degree and 4 being the greatest degree. Have them use the following criteria: Did I answer both questions? Are my ideas clearly stated?

B. How might the plot of this story be different if Martha were wealthy? What might be its new conflict and climax?

Student answers will vary, but should demonstrate knowledge of story conflict and

climax. They may mention that the principal might not have tried to change the rules

or that the jacket might not have been Martha's "only chance."

_____

_____

_____

_____

_____

_____

_____

Testing Plot

A. Read the passage below. Then read it a second time and write the word that best fills each blank. Be sure you keep the developing plot in mind as you read.

"Why does everyone continue to remind me to meet at Martin's house at 5:00," Li wondered.

He had just finished writing the paper for his science class. Now, he had to return the ____books____ to the
(1)
library. While at the ____library____, he would look for a
(2)
book on fixing bicycles. He wished that his friends would stop
____pressuring____ him. After all, if he can't fix the ____bike____,
(3)   (4)
he won't be able to go to Martin's.

He thought ahead to what he would do next. "I will need to take a shower ____before____ meeting everyone." Then he
(5)
asked himself, "What is so important anyway? We're just getting together to watch a movie."

But little did he know, the guys were actually planning a
____surprise____ party for his birthday one week early.
(6)

B. Write an ending for the story above. Remember that the climax should be the high point of the story. You might, for example, have Li show up covered in bicycle grease. Make sure that the events you write work toward your resolution.

Student answers should reflect an understanding of story plot. They may mention

that Li misses his party or is unable to shower before going to meet his friends.

_____

_____

_____

_____

_____

Test-Taking Hints:
Remind students to read the passage twice: The first time to see what happens and the second time to make their choices.

1. (books)
   paper
   bike

2. bike shop
   store
   (library)

3. (pressuring)
   helping
   making it
   easy for

4. paper
   (bike)
   library door

5. after
   (before)
   while

6. dinner
   beach
   (surprise)

Unit THREE

BECOMING AN ACTIVE READER

Effective readers are active readers. They think about how their lives are similar to the lives of the people they read about in a **biography**. Then they decide how to use what they have learned in their own life. Good readers learn from others' experiences, and from their own.

Using Skills and Strategies

Asking questions about the information included in a biography will help you understand the **author's viewpoint**. You may ask: What facts has the writer included? What quotes have been chosen? Does the subject sound like someone you would like to know?

Authors often use **multiple meaning words**, or words that have more than one meaning. If the meaning you know for a word doesn't make sense in a sentence, you may ask: Do other words near this word provide clues to the word's meaning?

In this unit, learning to identify the **author's viewpoint** and to understand **multiple meaning words** will help you read biographies actively.

The Biography: The Writer's Voice

Biographies from all cultures instruct and entertain us. What can we learn from reading biographies? We can learn about other cultures. We can learn how other people think and talk. We can learn others' customs and values. Biographies can take us on vivid journeys to new worlds.

Responding to Biographies

Good readers observe the feelings and problems that people share. They also see new ways of thinking and behaving. It will be helpful to note these similarities and differences as you read "Xuxa: the Brazilian Sensation" and "Billy Mills." Writing sidenotes will help you become involved with these subjects. Use your notes during discussions with classmates.

Unit Enrichment: Have students write biographies about individuals they admire. The subjects may be nationally famous, local heroes, or simply a person the student knows and admires. Suggest that students focus their task by concentrating on one aspect of their subject's life and limiting their biographies to three pages. Publish the students' work in a volume entitled "Portraits."

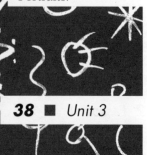

Author's Viewpoint

Lesson 5	Introducing page 39	Practicing page 40	Applying page 41	Reviewing page 51	Testing page 52

Introducing Strategies

A **biography** is a portrait of a person that is drawn in words instead of pictures. When good readers read a biography, they look for clues to the writer's **viewpoint**, or attitude toward the subject. Knowing the author's viewpoint helps you interpret and understand the biography. The diagram below shows you specific things to notice to help you determine the author's viewpoint.

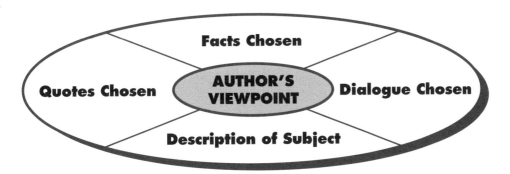

Reading the Biography

Read "Xuxa: the Brazilian Sensation" on pages 45-47 and the sidenotes on pages 45-46. These notes show what one reader discovered about the author's viewpoint. After you have finished reading, answer the questions below.

1. What does the reader think the author's viewpoint is about Xuxa?

Students should state that the reader identifies the author's viewpoint as positive.

2. What details from the biography does the author use to come to this conclusion?

Students might suggest details like calling Xuxa *the Brazilian Sensation* and the

discussion of her children's films show that the author creates a positive picture

of Xuxa.

Lesson Objective: To identify author's viewpoint by analyzing clues in biographies "Xuxa: the Brazilian Sensation" and "Billy Mills."

ESL/LEP: Make available some simple political cartoons. Ask students to work with partners to talk about the cartoons. Help students recognize how the pictures and words illustrate the cartoonists' viewpoints.

Modeling the Strategy: Read aloud a passage from a newspaper article to model identifying the author's viewpoint. Look for a passage that includes as many of the four items on the wheel as possible. After completing the page, use the Reproducible Activity master on page T14 of the ATE to help students apply the strategy to "Xuxa: The Brazilian Sensation."

Managing the Lesson: Remind students to use the sidenotes on pages 45-46 to model the process of active reading and to help them answer questions 1 and 2.

Practicing *Author's Viewpoint*

A. Read each passage below, then circle the letter of the choice that best completes each statement. On the line that follows, explain your choice.

1. The tall, blonde, blue-eyed actress was born in Santa Rosa, Brazil, on March 27, 1963. Her grandparents were from Austria and Italy.

   This passages provides
   a. clues to the biographer's viewpoint.
   b. a helpful quote.
   c. factual information.

   These details are all facts and can be proved.

2. Xuxa is more than a rich, beautiful, world-famous superstar, however. She is also a deeply caring person.

   This passages provides
   a. a description that gives clues to the biographer's viewpoint.
   b. dialogue that gives clues about the author's viewpoint.
   c. factual information.

   These adjectives suggest that the author's viewpoint is positive.

3. Xuxa also dances with an all-girl group, the "Paquitas," who try to copy Xuxa's trendy look.

   This passages provides
   a. facts that give clues to the biographer's viewpoint.
   b. a description of Xuxa.
   c. a quote that gives clues to the author's viewpoint.

   Students may suggest that the fact that the girls copy Xuxa shows she is popular.

B. If you were going to write a biography, who would your subject be? What would your viewpoint about this subject be?

Accept all appropriate responses. Students may choose subjects whom they know

personally or famous subjects representing a variety of media. Encourage students to

write a sentence that describes their viewpoint. Students should include dialogue,

facts, and a description that clearly illustrate their viewpoint.

Purpose: The purpose of this page is to help students practice identifying the author's viewpoint in the biography. Questions reflect the strategy illustrated in the wheel on the **Introducing** page.

Individualized Learning: Have students complete the page independently. Make sure that their explanations for Section A support the items they circled.

Cultural Awareness: Tell students that the samba is a popular Brazilian dance. Invite them to discuss popular dances from other cultures.

Writing Process: Students might choose to develop their response into a full biography as a total writing process activity.

Applying **Author's Viewpoint**

A. Read this excerpt from a biography about a painter, and then answer the questions that follow.

The bold, bright colors and odd lines in Miranda's portraits seemed strange to many people. Only she felt her paintings belonged on a museum wall alongside Picasso's. And she was right.

It took a lot of nerve—more nerve than you can imagine—to carry out her plan. Miranda entered the Rinaldi Art Gallery, a famous art gallery in New York. Mr. Rinaldi stood in the center of one room. Miranda introduced herself and handed him several slides that showed her paintings. As Miranda later wrote in her journal, "He took one look and smiled. A big smile!" Rinaldi recalls telling her, "Miranda, this is the beginning of a beautiful art career."

1. Describe the author's attitude toward the subject of the biography.

Students may suggest that the author uses facts and quotes to show a positive picture

of Miranda, who seems to be an admirable and talented artist.

2. List two details from the biography that support your opinion.

Students might suggest: "Only she felt her paintings belonged on a museum wall

alongside Picasso's. And she was right." and "It took a lot of nerve."

B. On the lines below, write a few sentences about Miranda. Use a different viewpoint from the one used by the author of this biography.

Suggest to students that they begin their response with a description of Miranda that

gives clues to their viewpoint. Encourage them to invent facts and quotes that support

their viewpoint. Point out that some sentences should reveal their feelings toward

the subject.

Applying the Skill to Everyday Reading: Students can practice identifying the author's viewpoint in stories, poems, and nonfiction they read in school and on their own. Have students describe how they figured out the author's viewpoint.

Cooperative Learning: Have students complete Section A in groups of three. One student should be the reader, another the moderator, and the third the recorder. Tell students there should be a consensus on their responses.

Conferencing: Have students work with a peer to analyze their use of viewpoint and the clues that help them identify it.

To review

↓

page 51

Multiple Meaning Words

| **Lesson 6** | Introducing *page 42* | Practicing *page 43* | Applying *page 44* | Reviewing *page 53* | Testing *page 54* |

Lesson Objective: To identify multiple meaning words and use context to figure out their definitions in the biographies "Xuxa: The Brazilian Sensation" and "Billy Mills."

Modeling the Strategy: Read aloud a passage from students' classroom texts to model using context to define multiple meaning words. Refer to the diagram as you work through the strategy. After completing the page, use the Reproducible Activity master on page T15 of the ATE to help students apply the strategy to "Xuxa: The Brazilian Sensation."

Oral Language: Explain that students often use multiple meaning words. Then pretend to prick yourself with a pencil point and say, "That point hurts!" Ask what the word *point* means in the sentence. Have students identify the context clues that help them define *point*. Then ask the students to identify other meanings for *point*. Invite volunteers to offer words that have multiple meanings. Then ask students to identify the words and their meanings.

Managing the Lesson: Remind students that they can use the multiple meaning words they have underlined in the biography to help them answer questions 1 and 2.

Introducing Strategies

Good readers know that a word can have **multiple meanings**, or more than one meaning. When they find a word that seems to have a meaning different from the one they know, they check the word's **context**, or the words around it that may give clues to its meaning. For example, the word *charge* can mean "an accusation," which does not make sense in the sentence "The charge up the steep hill was difficult for the horses." The dictionary, however, says that *charge* can also mean "an attack," which does make sense.

The diagram below shows how you can determine a word's meaning in context.

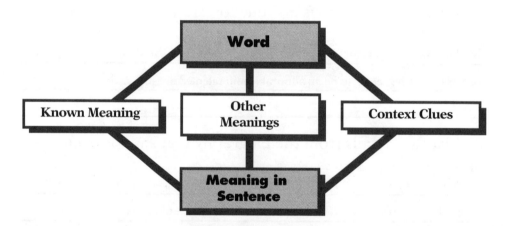

Reading the Biography

Reread "Xuxa: The Brazilian Sensation" on pages 45-47. Choose one page and underline all the words you find that have multiple meanings. Then complete the items below.

1. List two multiple meaning words in the selection.
Students may suggest: *fans, show, waves, bear,* and others.

_____

2. For each word you listed, write two sentences. Each sentence should use a different meaning of the word.
Students may suggest: Xuxa is supported by her *fans.* When it gets too hot, Xuxa

_____

fans herself.

_____

Practicing Multiple Meaning Words

A. In each sentence below, circle the letter of the item that correctly defines each underlined word. On the line that follows, explain your choice.

1. She entertained her many loving <u>fans</u> with songs, dances, stories, cartoons, and games.
   a. to blow air toward something or someone
   ⓑ people interested in something or someone
   c. something that stirs the air and cools
   d. to spread out like a peacock's tail
   Students might suggest that *loving* was the context clue used.

2. The <u>show</u> had a slow start on Manchete, Brazil's second-largest television station.
   a. to allow to be seen
   b. to explain and make clear
   ⓒ a performance or program
   d. a collection of items people can see
   Students might suggest that *television* gave them a context clue.

3. In a two-year <u>period</u> from 1989 to 1991, she earned $20 million.
   ⓐ an amount of time
   b. a punctuation mark
   c. portions of time in a game
   d. an end or conclusion
   Students might suggest that *1989 to 1991* gave them a context clue.

4. A <u>chain</u> of toy stores in Puerto Rico added small departments called "Xuxeria boutiques."
   a. series of related events
   b. something that binds, or holds back
   ⓒ restaurants or shops with the same owner
   d. fasten or lock away
   Students might suggest that *stores* gave them a context clue.

B. Look for multiple meaning words in the headlines of a newspaper or magazine. List at least two multiple meaning words, then write both of their meanings.

Encourage students to use a dictionary to find the multiple meanings of the words

they identify.

Purpose: The purpose of this page is to help students practice the skill of defining multiple meaning words in the biography. Questions reflect the response strategy illustrated in the diagram on the **Introducing** page.

Peer Sharing: Have students complete Section A with a classmate. Both partners should be able to explain their choices.

ESL/LEP: Show students a movie advertisement that contains multiple meaning words. Have them identify which words have more than one meaning and talk about their different meanings.

Individualized Learning: Have students complete Section B independently. They should check their work using a dictionary.

Applying Multiple Meaning Words

Applying the Skill to Other Disciplines: Students will notice that multiple meaning words appear in many books. For example, in a social studies text, *cell* might be "an enclosed space in a prison"; in a biology book, however, a *cell* is "a small part of a living organism." Have students list multiple meaning words they find in science, social studies, math, art, and other areas.

A. Read this paragraph from a biography about an artist. Then answer the questions that follow.

> Miranda received a letter on June 24th. It told her that she had won the National Art Award for a portrait of her father. She was in a state of shock. Immediately, she went into her studio and picked up a brush. Instead of painting on canvas, she picked up the coffee can in which all her brushes were stored. She began to paint the can, inside and out. She had not thought about it beforehand, but Miranda discovered a new idea for her painting. That was the beginning of her famous coffee can series.

1. Write a multiple meaning word that appears in the paragraph. Then write the word's meaning as it is used in the paragraph and another meaning for it.

Students might suggest: *letter:* a symbol from the alphabet; a written

personal message.

Cooperative Learning: Have students complete Section A in groups of three. One student should be the reader, another the moderator, and the third the recorder. Tell students there should be a consensus on their responses.

2. Explain how you figured out the meaning of this word.

Students might suggest that *received* and *June 24th* were context clues that helped

them know that Miranda received a written personal message.

3. Now write a sentence in which you use another meaning of the same word.

Students might suggest *My first and last names begin with the letter T* as a sentence

that uses another meaning for the word *letter*.

Conferencing: Have students compare lists and check the words in this timed response.

B. Write all the multiple meaning words you can think of in the next three minutes. Use a dictionary to check your list.

Encourage students to write any words that come to mind; they can check to make

sure the words have multiple meanings afterward with a dictionary. Students might

suggest: *pen, board, ruler,* and *tape.*

To review

↓

page 53

Julie Catalano enjoys writing for young people, especially about Latino issues. One of her books is *The Peoples of North America: The Mexican Americans.* Catalano has also contributed articles to a reference series called *Notable Hispanic American Women.* After writing this biography, she is eager to see Xuxa's new United States television series.

Xuxa: The Brazilian Sensation

by Julie Catalano

Maria da Graca Xuxa Meneghel grew up quite poor in Brazil. Today, she is known only as Xuxa (pronounced SHOO-shah) and she has been called Brazil's "Queen of Kid TV." Her name and face are among the most famous in Brazil. Every day from Monday to Saturday, millions of Brazilian children watch the "Xuxa Show." She entertains her many loving <u>fans</u> with songs, dances, stories, cartoons, and games.

◄ There's mostly factual information in this paragraph. I can't tell anything about the author's viewpoint yet.
Response Clue: Students might point out some of the multiple meaning words that are underlined in the text.

The tall, blonde, blue-eyed actress was born in Santa Rosa, Brazil, on March 27, 1963. Her grandparents were from Austria and Italy. They traveled to Brazil to make a new home. Her father was a Brazilian military officer. When she was seven, she moved with her family to Rio de Janeiro, the biggest city in Brazil. Her career started at age 16, when she was chosen to be the cover girl of a small magazine in Brazil. Her picture attracted so much attention that she was asked to <u>model</u> for more than 50 other magazines. Soon after, Xuxa became a model with the Ford Agency. This is one of the largest and most famous modeling agencies in the world.

◄ More factual information. I can't tell for certain how the author feels—but since she hasn't said anything negative, or bad, about Xuxa, maybe she likes her subject.

Xuxa made a series of children's films, including *A Blunderer in Noah's Ark*, and *The Blunderers and the Wizard of Oz.* She was then asked to host a television program for children in Brazil. The show had a slow start on Manchete, Brazil's second-largest television station. Xuxa then moved her show to Globo, the country's number one television network. By 1992, the "Xuxa Show" was the highest-rated daytime television program in Brazil. Her show now reaches about 50 million viewers each week in 15 countries.

◄ The author lists lots of Xuxa's successes. She must be proud of her achievements.

Both boys and girls love Xuxa's dazzling style. She sings, plays games with the children, reads letters aloud from her fans, and shows cartoons. Her studio audience often cheers, <u>waves</u> pompoms and throws confetti. Xuxa also dances with an all-girl group, the "Paquitas," who try to copy Xuxa's trendy look.

For many Brazilian children, Xuxa is more than just a fad. She is a big part of their childhood. To explain her success, Xuxa noted, "I try to create fantasies and help people to dream." For many Brazilian children, their biggest dream is to be on Xuxa's show.

The "Xuxa Show" is a mixture of reality and make-believe. Fairy tales are followed with serious stories. In addition, Xuxa talks to children about subjects such as ecology, health, geography, and world cultures. Many children view her as a mother and teacher. She always reminds her *baixinhos* (little ones) to be good, stay off drugs, care for the environment, and believe in themselves.

Xuxa is Brazil's number one recording artist. Her six albums in Spanish and Portuguese have sold more than 15 million copies, and her live concerts attract up to 40,000 fans.

She is also a very successful businesswoman. Her company, Xuxa Producoes, licenses about 50 products. In 1991, sales on those products totaled $52 million. Toys, clothing, books, shampoo, bicycles, and other products <u>bear</u> her name. When a <u>chain</u> of 24 toy stores in Puerto Rico added small departments called "Xuxeria boutiques," the Xuxa doll became the top seller. The toy industry has sold more than one million Xuxa dolls in the South American market. In the publishing field, there is a children's dictionary and a monthly magazine. More than

35 million Xuxa comic books have been sold. Each time Xuxa has appeared on the cover of *Gente*, Argentina's weekly magazine, 90 percent of its 130,000 issues have been sold.

Her show, recordings, books, and products have made Xuxa one of the richest entertainers in the world. In a two-year period from 1989 to 1991, she earned $20 million. She was the first Latin American to be on the *Forbes* magazine list of the 40 highest paid entertainers. She has a reported net worth of $100 million.

Xuxa is more than a world-famous superstar, however. The attention she gives to children, both on and off the screen, is widely recognized. She has taken part in anti-drug movements and public information programs on AIDS geared to young people. One of her most successful efforts was the Brazilian polio vaccination drive in 1989. Her public service announcements resulted in 90 percent of Brazilian children being immunized against polio. Because she knows that so many children look up to her, Xuxa does not smoke or drink. She is also a vegetarian.

To show her concern for those in need, Xuxa set up the Xuxa Meneghel Foundation. Money from the foundation has provided food, housing, and schooling for 250 Brazilian children. When the Brazilian Assistance Legion asked Xuxa to help collect food for poor children, more than 550 tons of food was sent. She has also given time and a large part of the money she earns from her licensed products to several important causes worldwide.

An English-language version of Xuxa's show is planned for the United States for the 1993-94 television season. The 30-minute shows are to be aired in New York, Los Angeles, Chicago, Philadelphia, San Francisco, Boston, and Washington, D.C. Songs, dance, games of skill and knowledge, and special guests will be included. The series has been designed to educate, inform, and entertain children aged two to eleven. Sixty-five episodes are planned for the first season, with more than 100 children in the studio audience at every show.

In 1987, the French newspaper *Liberation* included Xuxa in the list of outstanding women of the year. Her name appeared alongside such respected names as Raisa Gorbachev, the former First Lady of the Soviet Union, and Margaret Thatcher, the former prime minister of England. In 1991, *People* magazine named Xuxa one of the world's most beautiful people. Millions of children the world over would definitely agree.

ESL/LEP: Ask students to describe in their own words activities a Xuxa show might include.

Response Clue: Here the author emphasizes Xuxa's generosity. Students might note that the author views her subject favorably.

Clarification: You may wish to have students reread this paragraph to clarify that Xuxa uses part of her earnings to help children. Invite students to relate this information to the author's viewpoint.

Response Clue: Students who have difficulty recognizing multiple meaning words may want to highlight the words *season* and *aired*, identify the meaning used in this paragraph, and find additional meanings.

Cultural Awareness: Have students add names of outstanding women from different cultures around the world to those mentioned in this paragraph.

If you are working on

Lesson 5	Lesson 6
↓	↓
page 39	page 42

Susan Arkeketa teaches writing at Haskell Indian Junior College, the school that Billy Mills attended at age 14. Arkeketa, an Otoe-Creek who grew up in Tulsa, Oklahoma, met Billy several times when he visited Haskell to speak to students about meeting life's challenges.

Billy Mills

by Susan Arkeketa

The world's best distance runners were about to start the grueling run. No one at the Olympics thought that Billy Mills, a 26-year-old Oglala Lakota from Pine Ridge, South Dakota, could win. No one, that is, except Billy.

Billy Mills crouched down, putting his body, hands, and feet in place. He was about to begin the race of his life. The event? It was the 10,000-meter run at the 1964 Olympic games in Tokyo, Japan.

What led up to this special time in Billy Mills's life? On October 14, 1964, none of the more than 80,000 spectators watching the race knew of the lifetime of challenges that Billy had faced. The crowd didn't know that he already had beaten the odds just by being there. Billy had grown up on the Pine Ridge Indian Reservation. His mother died when he was 7. His father, who had encouraged Billy to go to school to make a better life for himself, died when he was 13. At the age of 14, Billy started school at Haskell Indian School in Lawrence, Kansas.

When Billy first entered Haskell, he weighed only 104 pounds and stood five feet, two inches tall. He decided to become a runner and build his strength. As his training progressed, Billy's coach recognized his potential. His coach became like a father to Billy, helping him study and encouraging him to run.

Running seemed to come naturally for Billy. At Haskell, he won the state two-mile cross country championships and the mile title. Other coaches and runners noticed Billy. The University of Kansas offered him an athletic scholarship, which he accepted.

In college, Billy almost called it quits. He was shy and often felt discouraged. He was living 600 miles from home, far from those who loved and supported him. In addition, prejudice from other students prevented him from joining clubs at the college. Mills felt like an outsider. He needed to decide whether to stay in college or leave.

After much thought, Billy decided to stay in college and meet the challenge. At Kansas, he ran his first 10,000-meter race. He helped the University of Kansas win the National Track and Field Championships and the Big Eight cross country championship. He was named an All-American three <u>times.</u>

Meeting Individual Needs: Have students who are having difficulty identifying the author's viewpoint review this paragraph, which describes the subject positively. Suggest they write their own sidenote about author's viewpoint here.

Billy graduated from the University of Kansas. He then married his college girlfriend and joined the Marine Corps as a commissioned officer. He thought his running days were over.

Then a fellow officer persuaded Billy to run again. Billy started his training and competed in military <u>track</u> and field <u>meets</u>. He won the 10,000-meter run in Germany, and the Marines sent him to the Olympic <u>trials.</u> There he qualified for the 10,000-meter run.

At this point in his life, Billy had accepted the challenges of poverty, school, and distance running. The 1964 Olympic Games gave him another challenge. He met it with the run of his life.

Response Clue: Students might point out that based on the facts in this paragraph, the writer believes Billy was a person who accepted and met challenges.

The favorite runners in the Olympic event were Ron Clarke of Australia, who had set the world record earlier that year, and Mohammed Gammoudi from Tunisia. Billy definitely was not a favorite.

On the bus <u>trip</u> to the Olympic stadium, a fellow Olympic hopeful asked Billy, "Who do you think will win, Ron Clarke or Mohammed Gammoudi?"

He told her, "Neither. I'm going to win."

At 4:30 P.M., the starting gun fired. Billy started the race from Lane 9, the lane reserved for the slowest

Response Clue: Students might note that the author chooses dialogue that reveals his subject's confidence and determination.

Response Clue: Students might identify the multiple meaning words underlined here.

Meeting Individual Needs:
For students who have difficulty identifying multiple meaning words, have them highlight the words *point* and *lap*. Then have them find the different meanings for each word in a dictionary and identify the one used in each of these sentences.

Response Clue: Students can relate the direct quotes in this paragraph about the hard work and effort of Billy Mills to the author's viewpoint about the subject.

Cultural Awareness: You might wish to locate the Black Hills of South Dakota on a map and explain that this land is sacred to its Native American inhabitants. Explain that after gold was found in these hills, the American government sent soldiers, including Custer, to take control of the land.

Response Clue: The sentences in this paragraph give clues to the author's viewpoint with description, facts, and direct quotes. Suggest students write a sidenote using this information.

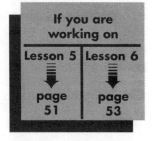

If you are working on

Lesson 5	Lesson 6
↓	↓
page 51	page 53

runners. After eight <u>laps</u> were completed, nine runners led the pack. Billy was one of them.

At the halfway <u>point</u>, Clarke led the race. Billy's lungs burned and his legs ached, but he did not give up.

The last <u>lap</u> for the gold medal lay straight ahead. Three runners—Clarke, Gammoudi, and Mills—struggled to take the lead. The pressure was almost unbearable. Suddenly, Gammoudi bumped into Clarke, who then bumped into Mills. The bump sent Billy into the third lane. He was now 20 yards behind!

In a flash, the words of his coach and his father came to mind: "Never give up." With new energy, he darted ahead and crossed the finish line. Sports announcers screamed out, "Billy Mills won! Billy Mills won!" His time was 28:24:4—an Olympic record. The crowd went wild. In all the excitement, Billy forgot to run his victory lap around the track.

When Billy returned to the United States, he was welcomed as a hero. On the Pine Ridge Reservation, the Oglala held a powwow to celebrate Billy's great deed. They presented him with a ring made of gold mined from the Black Hills in South Dakota. The Black Hills are sacred to the Oglala. Mills still wears his ring with pride.

Since winning the Olympics, Billy Mills has received much recognition. In 1972, the United States Junior Chamber of Commerce named him one of ten Outstanding Young Men in America. *Runners' World* magazine voted his race the most amazing upset in the history of U.S. distance running. A movie, *Running Brave*, was made about Billy's life on the Pine Ridge Reservation and his quest for the gold medal.

Billy Mills gives as much as he receives. He enjoys working with Native American youth. He started the organization called Running Strong for American Indian Youth. The organization awards scholarships and gives money to special projects on <u>reservations</u>. Billy also travels across the country speaking to young people. As he says, "Life is a series of challenges, and school is the best way you can help yourself to be ready to meet any challenges that come your way."

In 1984, Billy returned to Tokyo. He visited the stadium where he won the 10,000-meter race twenty years earlier. With his wife watching, Billy jogged around the track. Twenty years later, he finally took his Olympic victory lap.

Today, Billy owns his own insurance and public relations firm in Sacramento, California. He is active in civic and social organizations. And, yes, he still jogs.

Reviewing Author's Viewpoint

A. Read "Billy Mills" on pages 48-50. Use the wide margins to take notes about the author's viewpoint. Then use the diagram below to organize your ideas.

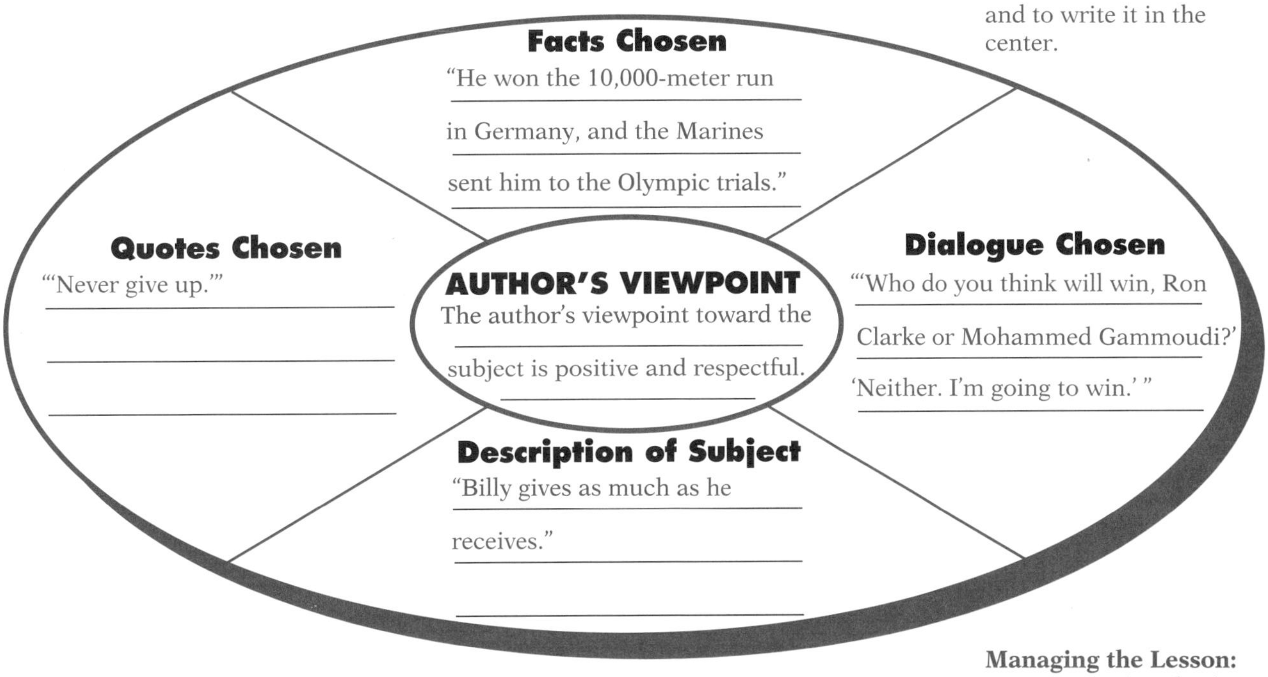

Reviewing the Strategy: Have students refer to the sidenotes they wrote on pages 48-50. Tell them to write details from the biography in the four outside sections of the wheel. Then ask students to determine the author's viewpoint based on these details and to write it in the center.

Facts Chosen
"He won the 10,000-meter run in Germany, and the Marines sent him to the Olympic trials."

Quotes Chosen
"'Never give up.'"
_____
_____

AUTHOR'S VIEWPOINT
The author's viewpoint toward the subject is positive and respectful.

Dialogue Chosen
"'Who do you think will win, Ron Clarke or Mohammed Gammoudi?'
'Neither. I'm going to win.'"

Description of Subject
"Billy gives as much as he receives."
_____
_____

Managing the Lesson: Answers on the wheel are suggestions. Students may cite other details.

B. On the lines below, write a paragraph about the author's attitude toward Billy Mills. Use the notes you have written in the margins and the diagram above for ideas and details.

Encourage students to include the information they recorded in the diagram to support the idea that the author's attitude toward Mills is positive, admiring, and respectful.

_____
_____
_____
_____
_____
_____
_____

Individualized Learning: Have students complete the paragraphs independently. Remind them to refer to the notes they have written on the wheel for examples.

Testing *Author's Viewpoint*

Test-Taking Hint: Tell students that when they take reading tests they sometimes have to decide whether or not a statement is true. Suggest that the students read each statement twice before making a choice. Then tell them to fill in the appropriate bubble completely. Remind them to use the strategy they have learned for identifying the author's viewpoint.

A. In the items below, fill in the bubble next to each true statement. On the lines that follow each item, explain your response.

● **1.** The author feels that Billy Mills faced many difficult challenges in his life.

Students should use an example or detail from the selection to explain this choice.

○ **2.** The author feels that Billy Mills's background made it easy for him to succeed.

On the contrary, Billy's life was full of hardship.

○ **3.** The author feels that Billy Mills did not deserve to win the Gold Medal.

On the contrary, the author shows that she thinks Billy deserves and has earned all

the recognition he has received.

● **4.** The author feels that Billy Mills is an excellent role model for young people.

Students should use an example or detail from the selection to explain this choice.

Assessing Student Writing: Rate student writing on a scale of 1-4, with 1 being the least degree and 4 being the greatest degree. Use the following criteria: includes relevant information, uses examples from the text, clearly expresses an opinion.

B. How do you feel about Billy Mills? How do you think the author's attitude or opinion influenced yours? Write your opinion in one or two sentences on the lines below.

Students might begin their paragraphs by clearly stating their opinion. In the rest of

the paragraph, they should include details from the selection to support their opinion

and discuss how the author's viewpoint influenced their own.

To begin Lesson 6

↓

page 42

Reviewing *Multiple Meaning Words*

A. Reread "Billy Mills" on pages 48-50. Choose one page and underline any multiple meaning words you find there. Use the strategy pictured below to figure out each word's correct meaning in context. Then choose one of these words and use it to complete the diagram.

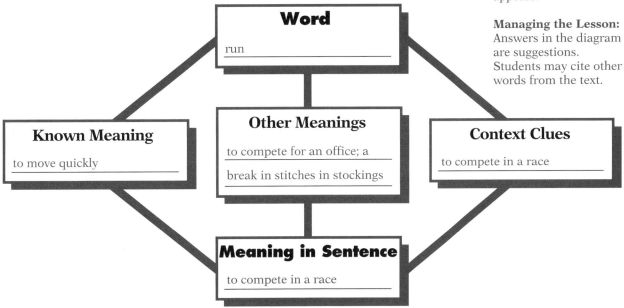

Word

run

Known Meaning

to move quickly

Other Meanings

to compete for an office; a

break in stitches in stockings

Context Clues

to compete in a race

Meaning in Sentence

to compete in a race

B. Choose another one of the multiple meaning words you found in the biography. Write the word's multiple meanings, then use each word in a sentence that shows its meaning.

Encourage students to apply the first steps of the strategy to find a word with multiple

meanings and to record the various meanings of it. Check to see that their sentences

correctly use the various meanings of the word.

_____

_____

_____

_____

_____

_____

Reviewing the Strategy: Have students refer to the words they underlined. Tell students to choose one multiple meaning word and write it in the box labeled *word*. They should then use context clues and analyze other meanings of the word to find its meaning in the sentence in which it appears.

Managing the Lesson: Answers in the diagram are suggestions. Students may cite other words from the text.

Individualized Learning: Have students complete the page independently. Make sure that for Section A they write the meaning of the word as it is used in the selection in the box labeled *meaning in sentence*. Encourage them to use a dictionary to check their response in Section B.

Testing Multiple Meaning Words

A. Read the passage below. Then think about the different meanings of each word in the list. Read the passage a second time and select the best word to fill in each blank. Then circle the word you have chosen and write it on the appropriate line.

1. (line)
   rope
   tape
2. ending
   (finish)
   final
3. toy
   cap
   (starting)
4. poor
   (latest)
   troubled
5. record
   coach
   (drive)
6. (flash)
   sign
   light

Test-Taking Hint: Tell students that on some reading tests they have to decide which word among three or four choices correctly completes a sentence. Remind students to think about the meaning of the sentence and the meaning of each choice. Since the time on reading tests is limited, remind students to pace themselves in order to complete the test. If they have trouble with a word, suggest they complete the test and return to the problem item if time permits.

All eyes were on the runners as they stepped up to the starting __line__ (1). Each athlete had one goal in mind—to reach the __finish__ (2) line first. The crowd was tense with excitement.

The blast of the __starting__ (3) gun sent the runners down the track. They seemed to fly past the cheering fans. In the outside lane, Billy Mills passed his first opponent. But the crowd didn't see him overtaking the runner. The fans were watching the favored distance runners, whose __latest__ (4) performances hinted that they might win today's race. Little did they know that Billy's __drive__ (5) would push him to victory. In a __flash__ (6) his father's words came to his mind, "Never give up." He didn't.

B. Look at each word that you selected above. Think about its different meanings. For each of the words you chose, write a sentence that uses a different meaning of the word.

1. The meanings of the words in student sentences should be different from their
2. meanings in the passage.
3. _____
4. _____
5. _____
6. _____

Unit *FOUR*

BECOMING AN ACTIVE READER

Good readers are active readers. They think about what the writer of an **autobiography** learned from experience. They then try to fit this information into their own lives.

Using Skills and Strategies

Identifying the **sequence** of events will help you keep track of what's happening in an autobiography. You might ask: What happened first? What happened next? Putting events in order helps you follow the path of a person's life.

One way authors bring you into a story is to describe a series of **causes** and **effects**. You may ask: What happened first? What was its effect? Did that effect cause something new to happen? Recognizing this chain of causes and effects can help you understand why events happen and predict what may happen next.

In this unit, learning to recognize the **sequence** of events and to identify **causes and effects** will help you read autobiographies actively.

The Autobiography: The Writer's Voice

An autobiography is an invitation into an author's culture. Readers see and hear the author's thoughts, feelings, and experiences. These may be familiar or they may be very different from the readers' own. As readers come to know other people and other cultures, they learn to both understand similarities and respect differences.

Responding to Autobiographies

Good readers often feel as if they have met the author of an autobiography. The story is personal and direct and can influence readers' thoughts and feelings. It is important to write your responses to the author as you read the excerpts from *This Life* and *The Land I Lost*. Writing notes will help you become involved with the writers and their stories. Use your notes as you discuss the autobiographies with your classmates.

Unit Enrichment: Invite students to write their autobiographies. First, have individuals brainstorm a list of events that they feel are significant. These events can be humorous or serious, but since students will be sharing their work, they may not want to select topics that are too personal. Encourage students to select one or two events and to list details about these events. Then have students write first drafts, share their writing with a partner, and revise their work. Finally, allow students to publish their autobiographies in a class book entitled "By Myself."

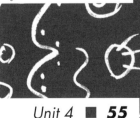

Sequence

Lesson Objective: To identify sequence in excerpts from the autobiographies *This Life* and *The Land I Lost* by outlining events in time order.

ESL/LEP: Display a panel drawing that shows a simple sequence of events. You might use illustrations from a cookbook or a "how-to" book. Ask students to tell a peer what is happening in each part.

Modeling the Strategy: Read aloud a passage from students' classroom texts to model identifying time sequence. Refer to the outlined order of events in the sequence chain. After completing the page, use the Reproducible Activity Master on page T16 of the ATE to help students apply this strategy to the excerpt from *This Life*.

Managing the Lesson: Remind students to use the sidenotes on pages 62-63. These notes will model the process of active reading and help students answer questions 1 and 2.

Introducing Strategies

When you put things in **sequence,** you put them in order. In a work of literature, a writer may arrange events in time sequence, that is, in the order in which the events happen. Paying attention to the order of events can help you follow the development of the action or argument. Some words that signal time sequence are *after, then, first,* and *next.*

Study the diagram below, which outlines the time sequence in one student's difficult morning.

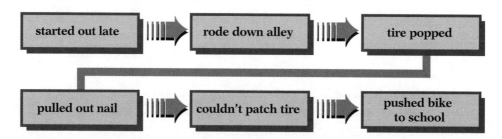

Reading the Autobiography

Read the excerpt from *This Life* by Sidney Poitier on pages 62-64 and the sidenotes on pages 62-63. The sidenotes show how one reader kept track of the order in which the events of the story happened. After you have finished reading, use these notes to answer the questions below.

1. List the sequence of events that the reader has found that describes how Sidney learned to drive.

First he watches the customers leave their cars. Next he watches the attendant. Then

he thinks he can drive but he cannot and is fired.

2. Which sequence words does the reader use in the sidenotes?

The reader uses the sequence words *first, next,* and *before.*

Practicing Sequence

A. Circle the answer that best completes each sentence below about the sequence of *This Life*. Then, on the line below each item, explain your choice.

1. After Sidney went downtown,

   a. he went to see a movie.
   ⓑ he watched people parking cars.
   c. he watched attendants washing cars.
   d. he got a job driving cars for wealthy people.

   This was the first thing Sidney did to get a job as a parking attendant.

2. Sidney would try to get a job at a new place, and then

   a. he would be asked to leave.
   b. he would become more confident.
   c. he would learn a little bit more about how to drive.
   ⓓ all of the above

   All these things happened after Sidney got a job at a new place.

3. After the first day, Sidney

   ⓐ had dented several cars.
   b. had a good job.
   c. had given up.
   d. had gotten his driver's license.

   Sidney did not learn to drive on his first day parking cars.

4. Finally, Sidney discovered that

   a. he was a pretty good driver.
   b. he would never be a good driver.
   ⓒ he was too young to get a license.
   d. there was no money to be made by parking cars.

   This is the reason Sidney stopped trying to get a job parking cars.

B. Sidney tried over and over again to get a job parking cars. Describe a similar experience that you, or someone you have read about or seen in a movie, has had. Be sure that you tell events in the sequence in which they happened.

Students should relate an experience in which they or someone else tried repeatedly

to learn a new skill. They should organize their work in time sequence. They might

use sequence words such as *first, second, next,* and *finally*.

Purpose: The purpose of this page is to help students practice identifying sequence in an autobiography. Questions reflect the strategy of outlining the order of events illustrated in the sequence chain on the **Introducing** page.

Peer Sharing: Have students complete Section A with a classmate. Both partners should be able to explain why the other choices are incorrect.

Writing Process: Students might choose to develop their response into a total writing process activity.

Applying Sequence

Applying the Skill to Everyday Reading: Have students practice outlining a sequence of events as they read a recent newspaper or magazine article.

Cooperative Learning: Have students complete Section A in groups of three, with one student as reader, another as moderator, and the third as recorder. Groups might enjoy comparing their answers to question 2.

A. Read the passage below from the autobiography of opera singer Marian Anderson. Pay attention to the order in which things happen. Then answer the questions that follow. Use sequence words in your answers.

> *Suddenly I discovered the violin. I had heard someone play it, I no longer remember who—probably it was in church—and I thought it would be a fine thing to play that instrument.*
>
> *At this time I was beginning to earn some money. My first job was scrubbing the steps of our neighbors' houses. If you scrubbed a whole set of steps you could earn as much as five cents. I worked hard at it, making sure the steps I scrubbed were cleaner than the steps the other kids were scrubbing. At first I used the pennies for candy when we were allowed to have it, and for tiny contributions in Sunday school. Then I began to save. I also ran errands. We had a lot of company at our house, and sometimes a visitor gave me a nickel or a dime. After a while I had four dollars. It was time to buy a violin.*

1. List the steps that Marian Anderson takes to buy a violin.

First she scrubs steps, then she decides to save her money, finally she runs errands.
_____

_____

2. What do you think happened between the time Anderson began running errands and the time she bought the violin?

Students may suggest that she thinks about the money she is earning and decides she

can save it for something special.

ESL/LEP: After students have written their response to Section B, have them present their directions to the class. Students might use diagrams or props to help them explain the steps in the process.

B. Choose something you know how to do, such as creating a hairstyle, changing a tire, or preparing a recipe. Write directions so somebody else can do it. Be sure your directions are in the proper sequence.

Students should discuss the process of completing some activity in time sequence.
_____

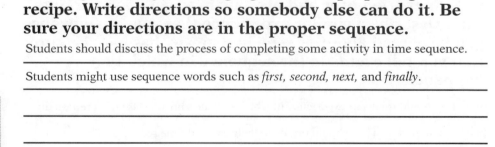

Students might use sequence words such as *first, second, next,* and *finally*.
_____

_____

_____

_____

To review

page
67

Cause and Effect

Introducing Strategies

A **cause** is an action or event that brings about a result. This result is called the **effect**. For example, you flip a switch, and the light comes on. Flipping the switch is the *cause*; the light coming on is the *effect*.

Writers of both fiction and nonfiction often describe what happens through a series of causes and effects. In this way, the reader sees how one action or event causes another one. The cause-and-effect chain below shows how one action can influence many other events.

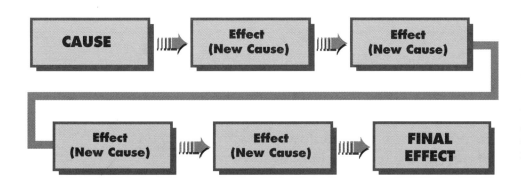

Reading the Autobiography

Reread the excerpt from *This Life*, on pages 62-64. As you read, draw arrows between the causes and effects you find. For example, Sidney did not know how to drive (the cause), so he had an accident (the effect). When you have finished reading, answer the questions below.

1. List three causes and effects you found in *This Life*.

Students may suggest: Because he strips the gears in a car, the manager fires him; he

doesn't want to try places too close together, so he walks 5 or 6 blocks; he wrecks a

car, then is fired.

2. How would this story have been different if Sidney Poitier had decided to get his license first?

Students may note that Sidney may have kept his first job, but he wouldn't have

learned about trying harder in the face of challenge.

Lesson Objective: To identify cause and effect in the excerpts from *This Life* and *The Land I Lost* by creating a cause-and-effect chain.

ESL/LEP: Have a student volunteer pour a few drops of green food coloring into a glass of milk. Ask students to tell a peer what happens and why.

Modeling the Strategy: Read aloud a passage from students' texts to model identifying cause and effect. Refer to the cause-and-effect chain. After completing the page, use the Reproducible Activity Master on page T12 of the ATE to help students apply this strategy to the excerpt from *My Life*.

Managing the Lesson: Remind students that they can use the arrows they have drawn between causes and effects to help them answer questions 1 and 2.

Practicing *Cause and Effect*

A. Each pair of statements below contains a cause and its effect. In each pair, circle the letter of the cause. Then, on the line below each one, explain your choice.

Purpose: The purpose of this page is to help students practice identifying causes and effects in an autobiography. Questions reflect the strategy of creating a cause-and-effect chain illustrated on the **Introducing** page.

Individualized Learning: Have students complete the page independently. Make sure that their explanations for Section A support the items they have circled.

1. (a) Sidney wants to earn money.

    b. Sidney applies for jobs parking cars.

Sidney's desire to earn money causes him to try to get a job parking cars.

2. a. Sidney runs into something.

    (b) Sidney figures out how to use the clutch, but nothing else.

Sidney's limited knowledge of driving causes several disastrous effects.

3. (a) Sidney gets more experience driving a car.

    b. Sidney manages to stay employed for a whole day.

Sidney's increased experience causes him to stay on a job for a whole day.

4. (a) Sidney feels he is ready for a driver's license.

    b. Sidney goes to the License Bureau.

Sidney goes to get a license because he feels he has parked enough cars.

5. a. Sidney is turned down for a driver's license.

    (b) Sidney is 15 years old.

Because Sidney is too young, he cannot get a license.

Conferencing: Have students conference with a peer to identify the causes and effects in each other's responses.

B. Imagine you are walking down the street and you find either a wallet full of money or a lost dog. Write a paragraph in which you describe what you do. Circle the causes and the effects of your actions.

Student responses should reflect an understanding of cause and effect. Students who

write about finding the wallet may discuss taking it to a police station and later

getting a reward. Students who write about finding the dog may discuss taking it

home, phoning the number on the dog tag, returning it to the owner, and seeing a

child's happiness when the dog is returned.

Applying *Cause and Effect*

A. Read the passage below taken from *Black Elk Speaks*, by John G. Neihardt. This book is an account of what happened at Wounded Knee, South Dakota, in 1890, between a band of Lakota and the U.S. Army. After you have finished reading, answer the questions that follow.

Some [Lakota] had not yet given up their guns, and so the soldiers were searching all the tepees, throwing things around and poking into everything. There was a man called Yellow Bird, and he and another man were standing in front of the tepee where Big Foot was lying sick. They had white sheets around and over them, and eyeholes to look through, and they had guns under these. An officer came to search them. He took the other man's gun, and then started to take Yellow Bird's. But Yellow Bird would not let go. He wrestled with the officer, and while they were wrestling, the gun went off and killed the officer.

1. What causes the officers to search the tepees?
Some Lakota have not turned in their guns, so the soldiers are searching for them.

_____

_____

2. Explain the causes of the officer's death.
The officer tries to take the gun, but Yellow Bird refuses. They struggle and the gun
_____
goes off, killing the officer.
_____

_____

B. Think of an argument that you have been in, or one that you saw on television or in a movie. List the cause or causes of the argument and its effects.
Students will need to clearly state the cause or causes of an argument and its effects.
_____
Some of the effects may, in turn, be causes that result in other effects.
_____

_____

_____

_____

_____

_____

Applying the Skill to Other Media: Tell students that tracking cause and effect in TV dramas can help them understand the story. Ask students to describe a program they have seen and to chart for the class the causes and effects that occurred. Students can draw their cause-and-effect chain on the board.

Peer Sharing: Have students complete Section A independently, then work with a partner to compare answers. Encourage students to make sure their partners provide details from the passage to support their answers.

Writing Process: Students might choose to develop their responses to Section B into the first draft of a short story or autobiographical sketch, then expand their work into a total writing process activity.

To review
↓
page
69

Preteaching Vocabulary:
You may wish to preteach the following vocabulary words: *attendant, triggered, accelerator, references, perception.*

Motivating Question: Ask students to list jobs they think teenagers can do well.

Sidney Poitier (1927-   ), born in Miami, Florida, was raised in the Bahamas. Returning to the United States as a teen, he decided to become an actor. Hard work and determination resulted in his becoming one of the first African Americans to get leading roles in Broadway plays and major movies. This humorous excerpt from his autobiography tells about a job he decided to pursue before acting.

from This Life

by Sidney Poitier

The notes in the margin show what one reader noticed about the order, or sequence, of events in the selection.

. . . I decided that I wanted to park cars because everywhere I went I saw parking lots with signs saying "Attendants wanted." Moreover, it seemed like quite a glamorous job in those days to be an attendant zipping around in all those different cars. My only difficulty was that I hadn't the faintest idea how to drive. I went downtown to a car park place and stood at the little hut where customers drove up and turned their cars over to the attendant. I stood there looking directly into the cars

First Sidney watches what the customers do. Can he learn anything this way?

and saw exactly what the customers did when they left their cars. Then I looked into the window at the attendant who was parking the car, to see exactly what he did with

Next he watches the attendant.

his hands and his feet. I concentrated on the hands first and memorized the sequence of movement that triggered the car into motion. Next I made mental note of every movement made with his feet, however slight. After a while I thought: I can do that—it's just a matter of coordinating the hands and feet. Yes indeedy, I'm ready to

I can't believe he thinks he's ready to drive.

Response Clue: The circled words represent causes; the underlined words are effects. Students might note, for example, that Sidney goes to another parking lot because he thinks he has learned to park cars by watching someone else.

give it a shot. So I went to another place that had a sign hanging out. I walked in and said, "I've come to see about the job." They said, "Can you drive?" "Yes, I can drive." "Do you have a license?" "Yes, I have a license." They said, "Fine. Take that car and put it in the slot over there." I said, "Certainly." I walked over, got into the car, put it in reverse, and right away began stripping the gears. The guy ran over and grabbed me out of the car and almost beat me, he was so angry, but finally he just shooed me

Sidney is thrown out. How could he think he could park cars before he learns to drive?

away. I went another five or six blocks away, not wanting to try places too close together, walked into another place with a sign, and announced I was looking for a job. They said, "Where have you worked before?" I said, "Downtown at such-and-such a place." They said, "Okay, put away that car, over there." Now, I've learned you don't get into a car and put it in gear the way I did with the last

ESL/LEP: Help students clarify the meanings of such expressions as *triggered the car into motion, stripping the gears,* and *shooed me away.*

one. So I put my foot on the clutch and sure enough it's in first gear and it starts off—not jerky, kinda smooth, and I'm rolling along—but I panic because I don't know what to do after that. I kept it in first gear and suddenly I hit the brakes. The car jerks a little. I look around and there's the guy watching me kinda funny. So I turn the car toward an empty slot and as I do I run right into something—bang! I got thrown out of that place, too. But now I know two things you do—you ease up and press down on the accelerator ever so softly, and when you hit the brakes you don't have to crash down on them. I figure finesse is the name of this game, so here I go one more time.

By the time I go to the next place I know the whole protocol required to apply for a job at a place like this. I walk up with a lot more confidence—having got the other wrecks behind me—and there is a guy and his wife and I say, "I'd like to apply for a job." They both are busy parking cars and obviously need help. She says, "Do you have references?" I say, "I've worked in Coral Gables and Fort Lauderdale and I've been parking cars for a couple of years." He says, "Okay," and takes down my "particulars" (all made up on the spot). "You'll start over there and fill up that southwest area, and you must always park them with the front end to the wall. And back the next car against that one so that people can get out easily, and make sure that the keys are left in the car." In those days people weren't as afraid of their cars being stolen as they are today. Anyway, I get into a car and lo and behold, it's one of those foreign makes and I don't know what . . . to do with that car. I figure I'll have to take a chance, so I cross my fingers, press down on the clutch, turn the key, and the car jumps into life. By now, I know about finesse, so I push into a gear, ease up on the clutch, and noticing that the car has started off backward, I say, "Ah-ha! That's reverse." Then I get it into—maybe not first, but second. I take off and I'm driving, but before I can get the car where I'm supposed to park it, I crash into something, and again I get tossed away.

By now I've realized that my biggest fault is in depth perception. You're going to have to make your turns wider, I said to myself. You're going to have to realize that you're dealing with five feet behind where you're sitting, and you've got three or four feet ahead of you, therefore, you have to gauge how you're going to get that much hulk—rather than your own dimensions—into a particular space. Armed with this new insight, I moved

Meeting Individual Needs: For students who are finding it difficult to identify causes and effects, highlight the sentence that begins, "So I put my foot on the clutch. . . ." Then ask students if that action causes something else to happen (the car starts off "kinda smooth"). Finally, ask students what causes Sidney to panic ("because I don't know what to do after that").

He gets thrown out of this place, too. He seems to be learning to drive, but he's doing it in a very unusual way.

Now use the margins to write your own notes about the sequence of the events in the autobiography.

Response Clue: Help students see that words like *so, then, before, again,* and *now* help the reader understand the sequence of events. Students might write sidenotes about sequence when they see such word clues.

Response Clue: Ask students how they think Sidney feels each time he is "tossed away." Discuss the effect these actions had on him. Students might note that he just kept trying.

ESL/LEP: Help students understand the meaning of *armed with new insight*.

from *This Life* ■ **63**

Clarification: Have students discuss why Sidney was careful not to go to places that were too close together.

Response Clue: Students may conclude that Sidney is very determined to get a job when he returns the next day. His disappointments of the first day have not caused him to give up.

Response Clue: Students might position sidenotes about sequence near words like *the next day, so, again, by this time,* and *then.*

on in search of the next job. At the end of a single day, I had gone through six or seven places and I had wrecked six or seven cars. The next day I had to try a whole new area because I had wiped out an awful lot of cars and I think my reputation had preceded me in downtown Miami. So I went to a new place and worked there for a whole day before I got fired, which meant that I successfully parked a lot of cars before getting kicked out of there for not being smooth enough. The very next job I got I was driving, and driving very well—considering. Again, without much finesse, without much style, without much evidence of experience in the way I handled the cars; and again I was fired. But by this time I was a driver. I had learned how to drive on those parking lots with no lasting damage done except to the string of wrecks I left behind me. Then, now that I knew how to drive the realization hit me that I was going to need a driver's license if I was to hold a job in a parking lot or even work as a truck driver; either way, I needed a license. I rushed over to the License Bureau and discovered that at fifteen I wasn't old enough to get a license. That ended my driving career, and I started doing other things.

If you are working on

Lesson 7	Lesson 8
⬇	⬇
page 56	page 59

from The Land I Lost

by Huynh Quang Nhuong

When she was eighty years old my grandmother was still quite strong. She could use her own teeth to eat corn on the cob or to chew on sugar plants to extract juice from them. Every two days she walked for more than an hour to reach the marketplace, carrying a heavy load of food with her, and then spent another hour walking back home. And even though she was quite old, traces of her beauty still lingered on: Her hands, her feet, her face revealed that she had been an attractive young woman. Nor did time do much damage to the youthful spirit of my grandmother. . . .

One morning my grandmother wanted me to go outside with her. We climbed a little hill that looked over the whole area, and when we got to the top she looked at the rice field below, the mountain on the horizon, and especially at the river. As a young girl she had often brought her herd of water buffaloes to the river to drink while she swam with the other children of the village. Then we visited the graveyard where her husband and some of her children were buried. She touched her husband's tombstone and said, "Dear, I will join you soon." And then we walked back to the garden and she gazed at the fruit trees her husband had planted, a new one for each time she had given birth to a child. Finally, before we left the garden my sister joined us, and the two of them fed a few ducks swimming in the pond.

That evening my grandmother did not eat much of her dinner. After dinner she combed her hair and put on her best dress. We thought that she was going to go out again, but instead she went to her bedroom and told us that she didn't want to be disturbed. The family dog seemed to sense something was amiss, for he kept looking anxiously at everybody and whined from time to time. At midnight my mother went

Clarification: Point out that the narrator's saying, "It took me a long time to get used to. . . ." is a clue that some time has elapsed.

Response Clue: Students might note that the words *even now* and *many years later* help define the sequence of events.

Response Clue: Students may see the grandmother's death as a cause that has a lasting effect on the narrator.

to my grandmother's room and found that she had died, with her eyes shut, as if she were sleeping normally.

It took me a long time to get used to the reality that my grandmother had passed away. Wherever I was, in the house, in the garden, out on the fields, her face always appeared so clearly to me. And even now, many years later, I still have the feeling that my last conversation with her has happened only a few days before.

If you are working on

Lesson 7	Lesson 8
↓	↓
page 67	page 69

Reviewing *Sequence*

A. Read the excerpt from *The Land I Lost* on pages 65-66. Then use the sidenotes you have written about the grandmother's activities to complete the sequence chain below. Begin with the event that has been filled in for you and follow the arrows, listing an event in each box.

Reviewing the Strategy: To help students complete the sequence chain, have them refer to the sidenotes they wrote on pages 65-66. Tell students to use these notes to list an event in each box in the sequence chain.

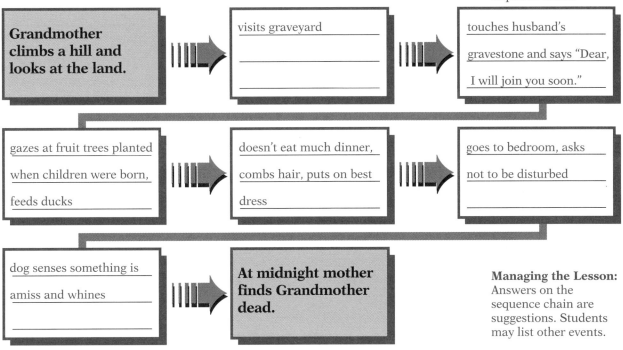

Grandmother climbs a hill and looks at the land.

visits graveyard _____

touches husband's _____ gravestone and says "Dear, I will join you soon."

gazes at fruit trees planted when children were born, feeds ducks

doesn't eat much dinner, combs hair, puts on best dress

goes to bedroom, asks not to be disturbed _____

dog senses something is amiss and whines _____

At midnight mother finds Grandmother dead.

Managing the Lesson: Answers on the sequence chain are suggestions. Students may list other events.

B. Think about a time when you or someone you know found something that was lost. List in time sequence the steps used to find the object.

Students should relate an event in time sequence. If students are uncomfortable

writing about a personal experience, encourage them to write about someone they

know or someone from a story they have read or a movie they have seen.

_____

_____

_____

_____

_____

Student Self-Assessment: Students might wish to evaluate their own writing on a scale of 1-4 with 1 being the least degree and 4 being the greatest degree. Have them use the following criteria: draws a clear picture of the process, develops sequence in chronological order, uses sequence words.

Testing Sequence

Test-Taking Hints:
Tell students that some tests will require that they put events into sequence. Suggest that they read all of the statements before they determine time sequence. Students should use details from the story to explain their answers.

A. Below are six statements about *The Land I Lost*. In the blanks, number the statements to show the order in which they happened. Then, on the lines below, explain your choices.

<u>4</u> The family dog senses something is wrong and whines from time to time.

The dog whines in the evening after Grandmother has gone to her room.

<u>2</u> Grandmother and the narrator's sister feed ducks swimming in a pond.

They feed the ducks after walking up the hill.

ESL/LEP: Some students may have difficulty writing explanations for their choices in Section A. In such cases, ask students to respond orally.

<u>1</u> Grandmother visits the graveyard where her husband is buried.

Grandmother does this after going up the hill with the narrator.

<u>3</u> After eating very little dinner, Grandmother combs her hair and puts on her best dress.

This happens after the events of the day.

<u>6</u> The narrator remembers his grandmother long after she is dead.

At the end of the story, the narrator talks about remembering his grandmother.

Individualized Learning: Have students check their work by comparing it to the sequence chain they completed on the **Reviewing** page.

<u>5</u> The narrator's mother finds that his grandmother has died.

She discovers at midnight that the grandmother has died in her sleep.

B. Think of something you read, or something that was read to you, which is still fresh in your mind. Describe the story's events in order. Then tell why the events remain so clear in your mind.

Students' retelling of their own memory should be clear, with events described in

chronological order. Students might use sequence words like *first, second, then, next,*

and *finally.*

_____

_____

_____

_____

To begin Lesson 8

⬇

page 59

Reviewing *Cause and Effect*

A. Reread the excerpt from *The Land I Lost* on pages 65-66. As you read, circle the causes you find and draw arrows to their effects. Then use your information to help you complete this chart.

Reviewing the Strategy: Have students review the causes they circled and the effects they underlined within the selection. Remind them to use that information to complete the cause-and-effect chain.

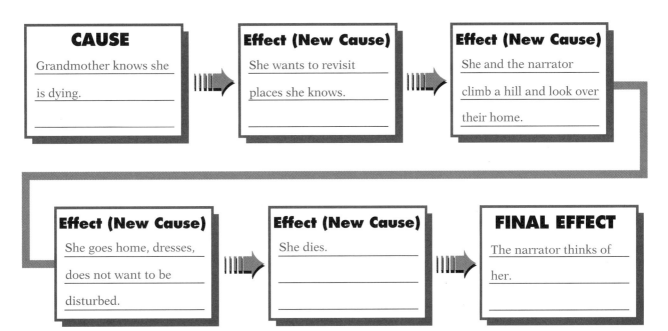

CAUSE

Grandmother knows she is dying.

Effect (New Cause)

She wants to revisit places she knows.

Effect (New Cause)

She and the narrator climb a hill and look over their home.

Effect (New Cause)

She goes home, dresses, does not want to be disturbed.

Effect (New Cause)

She dies.

FINAL EFFECT

The narrator thinks of her.

B. Name two or three qualities that cause the narrator to love and respect his grandmother.

Responses might include that Grandmother is strong physically and emotionally. She faces death bravely even though she obviously loves her world and her family. In old age she has inner and outer beauty.

_____

_____

_____

_____

_____

_____

_____

_____

_____

_____

Managing the Lesson: Answers on the cause-and-effect chain are suggestions. Students may find other causes and effects.

Assessing Student Writing: Rate student writing on a scale of 1-4, with 1 being the least degree and 4 being the greatest degree. Use the following criteria: names two or three qualities of the grandmother, uses supporting details from the text, and understands the relationship between the narrator and his grandmother.

Testing Cause and Effect

Test-Taking Hints:
Tell students that they should read each answer before choosing the one they think is best. Remind students that their explanations should include details from the story.

A. Circle the letter of the item that best completes each statement. Then, on the line below each one, explain your choice.

1. Grandmother tells her husband she will join him soon because
   a. she misses him.
   b. she is at his grave.
   c. she knows she will die soon.
   d. her grandson is with her.

   Knowing that she will die soon causes Grandmother to visit his grave.

2. Grandmother looks out over the field, mountain, and river because she
   a. is too tired to walk home.
   b. is taking a last look at the land she loves.
   c. is looking for the water buffalo.
   d. hopes to go swimming.

   Grandmother wants to see her home once again before she dies.

3. That evening, Grandmother puts on her best dress, and, as result, the family thinks
   a. she wants to have a family meeting.
   b. she wants to read to the children.
   c. she is going out.
   d. she is going to sing.

   The family thinks Grandmother is dressing because she wants to go out.

Student Self-Assessment: Students might wish to evaluate their own writing on a scale of 1-4, with 1 being the least degree and 4 being the greatest degree. Have them use the following criteria: Did I keep to the subject of the paragraph? Did I use examples from the text? Are my ideas clearly stated?

B. On the lines below, write a paragraph in which you describe how you think the narrator's memories of his grandmother will affect his life.

Responses will vary but should include some causes and effects. Students may suggest

that the narrator will try to learn from his grandmother's strength and inner beauty.

He may be inspired by her vigor to become physically strong. Because of her deep

love for her husband, he may be a devoted husband himself.

Unit FIVE

BECOMING AN ACTIVE READER

Critical readers are active readers. They question what they read in a **speech** and compare it to what they already know. If something is unclear, they stop and reread the confusing section. This review helps good readers make sure they understand the writer's message.

Using Skills and Strategies

Recognizing the **structure of a speech** will help you understand the points being made. You may ask: How does the writer introduce the topic? What details does the writer give to support or explain the topic? How does the summary help me check my understanding of the topic?

Good readers improve their vocabulary by learning **synonyms**, words with the same or nearly the same meaning, for words they know. They also learn **antonyms**, words with the opposite or nearly the opposite meaning, for words they know. They then try to use these new words when writing or talking to give their ideas variety.

In this unit, recognizing the **structure of a speech** and finding **synonyms and antonyms** for words you know will help you read more actively.

The Speech: The Writer's Voice

Speeches from all cultures inspire and entertain us. To do this, writers must get the attention of their listeners and their readers. They try to touch their readers' feelings—sometimes with fun, sometimes with thought. Readers often learn about other cultures by listening to the "voices" of their speakers.

Responding to Biographies

Good readers often imagine themselves in conversation with the writer. As you read, write notes about your own conversations with the writers of "Choose Your Own Life" and "Our Lands Are Sacred." Writing your comments in the margins will help you remember your thoughts as you discuss these speeches with your classmates.

Unit Enrichment: Show students videos of people making persuasive speeches. You might be able to obtain historical footage of such famous speakers as John F. Kennedy, Martin Luther King, Jr., and Winston Churchill. Discuss some of the techniques the speakers used, including gestures, variations of voice tone, and ways of making eye contact with the audience. Ask students to imagine which of these techniques the speakers in this unit might have used. Allow students to practice and present the speeches in this unit, applying the techniques you discuss.

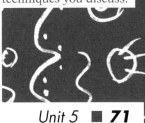

Structure of Speeches

Lesson 9	Introducing *page 72*	Practicing *page 73*	Applying *page 74*	Reviewing *page 83*	Testing *page 84*

Introducing Strategies

Speeches may be written for many different purposes. They may instruct, persuade, or inspire an audience. To achieve their purpose, writers of speeches organize what they want to say so that the audience can understand the points being made. A good speech is organized with a clear **beginning**, or introduction; **middle**, or body; and **end**, or conclusion. Each part serves an important purpose. The chart below shows how most speeches are structured.

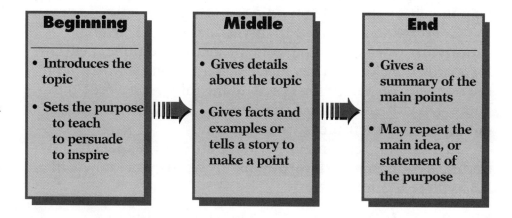

Beginning
- Introduces the topic
- Sets the purpose to teach to persuade to inspire

Middle
- Gives details about the topic
- Gives facts and examples or tells a story to make a point

End
- Gives a summary of the main points
- May repeat the main idea, or statement of the purpose

Reading the Speech

Read the speech "Choose Your Own Life" on pages 78-80 and the sidenotes on pages 78-79. The sidenotes show what one good reader noticed about the structure of the speech. After you have finished reading, answer the questions below.

1. What information does the reader find in the introduction, or beginning, of the speech?

The reader notes the use of a story as background information and the appeal to

readers' attention in the introduction.

2. What details does the reader use to guess what the body, or middle, of the speech might be?

The reader notes the organizing questions and the corresponding answers.

Practicing *Structure of Speeches*

A. Fill in the bubble next to the item that best completes each statement below. Then on the lines that follow, explain your choice.

1. Brenda Lane Richardson begins her speech by
   ○ telling a joke about junior high students.
   ● explaining why she will tell a story.

As a student, she didn't like speeches; she thought they were often boring. So she decided

to tell a story instead.

2. Early in the speech, we learn that Roach is dead. This detail
   ● makes us realize that this is a serious story.
   ○ gives away the ending of the story.

The speaker wants to grab the audience's attention and make listeners see she is

serious.

3. The middle of the speech is structured around three questions
   ○ asked by the writer of the speech.
   ● asked by Roach's mother after the funeral.

The mother is very upset and asks these questions to learn why this tragedy

happened.

4. Brenda Lane Richardson tells of her own life choices to get an education and be a writer
   ● in the end, or conclusion, of the speech.
   ○ in the middle, or body, of the speech.

She ends her speech by telling about her own decision to choose her own life.

B. Use the information in the speech to write a paragraph describing Brenda Lane Richardson's teenage years. Be sure your paragraph has an introduction, a body, and a conclusion.

Individual responses will vary, but students should structure their descriptions with a

beginning, a middle, and an end. They should also include facts about Richardson's

life, as mentioned in the speech, such as her refusal to join a girl gang, her habit of

carrying around a notebook, and her efforts to earn and save money for college.

Purpose: The purpose of this page is to help students practice recognizing the beginning, middle, and end of speeches. Questions reflect the strategy illustrated in the chart on the **Introducing** page.

Cooperative Learning: Have students complete Section A in groups of three. One student should read, one lead the discussion, and one record the group's responses to the items.

Peer Sharing: After students have completed Section B on their own, have them read their work aloud in groups. Group members should then identify each paragraph's parts.

Applying *Structure of Speeches*

A. Read the passage below, which is from the beginning of a speech. Then complete the items that follow it.

The sloppy condition of our school gym should be a matter of concern to all students at Hoover Junior High. It's our gym, and it's up to us keep it clean and safe.

1. Based on the introduction, what do you think is the purpose of this speech?

Students may suggest that the author is trying to point out problems in the gym's

condition and convince students to take action.

2. List at least three details that might be used in the middle of the speech.

Students should include specific details of conditions in the gym, such as used cups

left in the stands and equipment not put away, as well as specific suggestions for

correcting the problems, such as putting trash in a bin and storing equipment

properly.

3. On the lines below, write a brief ending for the speech.

Endings should summarize points made in the middle of the speech and could restate

the problem as defined in the beginning of the speech.

_____

_____

B. If you were asked to write a speech to deliver to your entire school, what would you write about? Jot down the purpose of your speech and list some points you might make in its beginning, middle, and end.

Students' responses will vary but should include a clearly stated purpose and have

ideas and points listed for the speech's beginning, the middle, and the end.

_____

_____

_____

_____

_____

Applying the Skill to Other Disciplines: Have students read a chapter from their social studies text. As they read, ask students to write sidenotes on a piece of notebook paper to note the structure of the chapter—its beginning, or introduction; its middle, or body; and its end, or conclusion.

Peer Sharing: Have students complete Section A with a classmate. Both partners should contribute ideas to the middle and end of the speech.

ESL/LEP: Encourage students to brainstorm their ideas aloud with a partner. They can then write their responses in an organized way on the page.

To review ⬇ page 83

Synonyms and Antonyms

Introducing Strategies

Good readers keep lists of words that interest them in their journals or reading logs. They then try to use these words in writing and conversation. Good readers also increase their vocabulary by thinking about the synonyms and antonyms of words. A **synonym** is a word that has a meaning that is the same or nearly the same as another word. An **antonym** is a word that means the opposite or nearly the opposite of another word. For example, *tired* and *exhausted* are synonyms; *tired* and *energetic* are antonyms.

Here's a strategy for finding and using synonyms and antonyms to build your vocabulary.

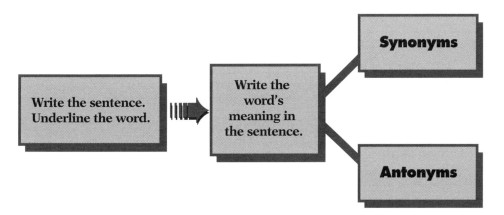

Reading the Speech

Reread "Choose Your Own Life" on pages 78-80. As you read, circle words for which you would like to learn synonyms or antonyms. Then complete these items.

1. Choose three of the words you have circled and then list at least two synonyms for each one.

Students may list words such as those circled in the speech and suggest synonyms

for each.
_____

_____

2. Choose three other words you have circled and list at least two antonyms for each one.

Students may list words such as those circled in the speech and suggest antonyms

for each.
_____

_____

Lesson Objective: To find and correctly use synonyms and antonyms in the speeches "Choose Your Own Life" and "Our Lands Are Sacred."

ESL/LEP: Bring in several sizes of cups and lids from a fast-food outlet. Ask students to describe the size of each one. Encourage them to use synonyms to describe the same sizes (*large, giant, huge*, etc.) and antonyms to describe opposite sizes (*small/big, wide/narrow*, etc.)

Modeling the Strategy: Read aloud a passage from the students' classroom text to model finding words that have synonyms or antonyms. Refer to the graphic organizer on this page. After completing the page, use the Reproducible Activity Master on page T14 of the ATE to help students apply the strategy to "Choose Your Own Life."

Managing the Lesson: Remind students that they can use the synonyms and antonyms they circled in the speech to help them answer questions 1 and 2.

Practicing Synonyms and Antonyms

A. In each pair of sentences below, write one synonym and one antonym for the underlined word. Then complete the sentences. On the line below, explain how your choice changes the meaning of the sentence.

1. The <u>brave</u> firefighter rescued the child from the burning building.

   Synonym: The ____heroic____ firefighter ____ran into the flames____.
   The firefighter's deed has become more remarkable.

   Antonym: The ____cowardly____ firefighter ____ran from danger____.
   A cowardly firefighter would stay away from danger.

2. The <u>small</u> child cried because she was lost.

   Synonym: The ____tiny____ child ____cried to be fed____.
   The child is younger and cannot care for herself.

   Antonym: The ____ten-year-old____ child ____found the door____.
   The change of size means that the child can see more clearly in a crowd.

3. The <u>loud</u> music kept all the neighbors up late.

   Synonym: The ____ear-piercing____ music ____gave us headaches____.
   The music has grown so loud that it causes pain.

   Antonym: The ____soft____ music ____lulled me to sleep____.
   The antonym changed the music from disturbing to soothing.

B. Brenda Lane Richardson describes Roach as both scary and kind. Write a paragraph about someone you know or have read about who also has such seemingly opposite qualities.

Responses will differ. Students may use synonyms and antonyms to describe a person

who is both cruel and kind, shy and friendly, or has some other seemingly opposite

qualities. Students who prefer not to write about an actual person may write about a

character in a book or movie.

Purpose: The purpose of this page is to help students practice finding and using synonyms and antonyms as they read and write. Questions reflect the strategy outlined in the graphic organizer on the **Introducing** page.

Managing the Lesson: Answers in Section A are suggestions. Students may list additional synonyms and antonyms and explain how each word change affects the meaning of the sentence.

Individualized Learning: Have students complete the page independently. Make sure that their explanations in Section A reflect their understanding of the meanings of the words they have used. Remind students that if they use a thesaurus, they should check their choices in a dictionary.

Writing Process: Students might develop their paragraphs from Section B into a rough draft for a longer story. They may then fully develop this work using the writing process.

Applying **Synonyms and Antonyms**

A. Read the following sentences. Then on the line below each item, tell whether the underlined words are synonyms or antonyms and explain how the words are similar or different.

1. It had been their <u>dream</u> to live in a free land, but achieving the dream turned into a <u>nightmare</u>.

The words are antonyms: a dream is usually pleasant; a nightmare is unpleasant.

2. Spencer <u>saved</u> every penny he earned that summer mowing lawns. By fall he had <u>accumulated</u> nearly enough money to buy a sleek mountain bike.

The words are synonyms: both mean "to collect."

3. As I interviewed my grandfather, I realized that his <u>recollections</u> were more than just <u>memories</u>. They were history.

The words are synonyms: both mean "remembered ideas."

4. The night was filled with <u>weird</u> hoots and shrieks. We had an <u>eerie</u> feeling that something strange was about to happen.

The words are synonyms: both mean "odd" or "unusual."

5. Sometimes I feel <u>clumsy</u> and think that I will never play basketball well. But when I'm "on," I feel as <u>graceful</u> as a butterfly.

The words are antonyms: *clumsy* means "awkward"; *graceful* means "attractive."

6. Marta noticed that sometimes her friends <u>neglected</u> the very people who <u>supported</u> them the most.

The words are antonyms: *neglected* means "did not take care of"; *supported* means "helped."

7. The class was eager to participate in the school's anti-drug campaign. Yoshi <u>promised</u> to create a poster and Kareem <u>pledged</u> to write a slogan.

The words are synonyms: Both refer to serious commitments to future actions.

B. Write a statement about something you like, such as a song, a movie, or a type of food. Then use at least one antonym to write a statement saying the opposite.

Students should choose an antonym for a key word in their first sentence in order to

make the statement express the opposite opinion.

Applying the Skill to Other Media: Remind students that synonyms and antonyms are often used in song lyrics. Synonyms allow a theme to be repeated, but with variety. Antonyms allow for rich contrasts. Ask students to find synonyms and antonyms in songs and change the lyrics by introducing antonyms.

Individualized Learning: Have students complete Section A independently. Make sure that their explanations of how the words are similar or different reflect the correct meanings of the words.

ESL/LEP: Encourage students to look up unfamiliar words in a dictionary in addition to looking for context clues.

Peer Sharing: Have students complete Section B with a classmate. Both partners should be able to identify the synonyms and antonyms used and explain the meanings of the words used.

To review

↓

page 85

Preteaching Vocabulary:
You may wish to preteach
the following vocabulary
words: *gagged, linings,
wounds, veil.*

Motivating Question: Have
students discuss the title of
the speech. Ask them what it
means to them to "choose
your own life."

Brenda Lane Richardson is an award-winning journalist. She
has co-authored a book, *Story Power: Talking to Teens in
Turbulent Times.* Richardson grew up in Brooklyn, New York.
She watched many of her friends—fellow African Americans as
well as those from other cultural groups—become involved in
gangs. In this speech she shares a personal experience that she
hopes will have a major impact on her teenage audience.

Choose Your Own Life

by Brenda Lane Richardson

The notes in the margins show what one reader noticed about the structure of the speech.

Yes, I've heard some boring speeches, too. Telling a story is a good way to get people to listen. This is a good beginning.
ESL/LEP: Help students see that *stayed on Roach's good side* means "tried not to make him mad."

The speaker is giving some background information in her introduction, too. I wonder what will happen to Roach. I think that will be the topic of the speech.

Response Clue: Some words for which students might wish to identify synonyms and antonyms have been circled.

Here's where the story takes off. You can tell the action is picking up. Something is going to happen to Roach. This worries me—he's like a lot of people I know.

Response Clue: You might encourage students to look for words, such as *nearby*, that are used more than once in close proximity. Suggest that they offer synonyms for these words.

▶ When I was in junior high, when my teacher gave me a speech to read or listen to, I gagged. That's why I decided that, rather than giving a speech, I'd tell you a story. The story is about a boy I knew when I was 12 years old. His name was Roach. Don't ask me how he got that name. He was big and he could be scary when he was angry. So most of the kids in my junior high stayed on Roach's good side. That meant they didn't ask too many questions.

▶ Don't get me wrong. Roach could be wonderful. If you were one of his many friends, he'd do anything for you. Once, when we were eating ice cream cones, I dropped mine. He made me take his. He pretended he didn't want any.

Maybe you've noticed that I talk as if Roach isn't around anymore. You're right. The last time I ran into him was in the eighth grade. I was on my way home one day when I saw him. I can still (picture) it.

▶ In those days, (cool) guys wore capes. (Go ahead, laugh if you like.) Roach ran past, and with his cape flying, he looked like a bird about to (soar.) I called his name, but he didn't wave. He was moving fast. Before I'd made it to the other side of the street, I heard the screams of 12 boys. I saw anger on their faces as they chased him.

I stood there, my back (pressed) into the wall of a (nearby) building. I was hiding, and I was worried about Roach. The Warlords, a gang from a nearby neighborhood, didn't kill Roach that day. He died two days later from wounds to his head, where they had kicked and stabbed him.

At his funeral that following week, everyone from his gang, the Bishops, came. They all wore black pants and shirts and capes with red linings. If it had been a movie, it would have been pretty. This was real life, though. His mother wore a hat with a veil and when they helped her outside, I heard her (moaning) these questions: Why had her son joined a gang? Why had someone hurt him? And what could Roach have done differently?

I'd like to share with you some of the answers I wish I could have given her that day.

Roach joined a gang because, even though he had lots of friends, he needed to belong to a family. His mother loved him and worked long, hard hours to support them. She was his only parent. With her being away so often, Roach wanted (just as every one of us does) to be a part of something that has a name and is respected.

I'll bet even 400,000 years ago, people who lived in caves grouped themselves off and promised to help one another. Being a member of such a group must have made life (easier). Say a woman had a stomachache from eating too much roasted bear meat. As a group member, she wouldn't have had to worry about getting a fire going that night. She could have warmed herself by the fire that the other members took turns building.

And so, still today, it is natural to want to belong to a family you can count on. It's true that street gangs, like Roach's, cause a great deal of harm and unhappiness. But for someone who feels alone and misunderstood, gangs can meet some important needs. For example, members often wear the same kind of clothes. This way, anyone who sees them knows they are (deeply) cared about by others who will do anything to protect them.

That promise must have sounded really good to Roach, who had lots of friends but no real family. It must have felt great for a while, to belong and to walk down the street with his head held high, knowing he was (respected.)

What did it feel like to be hunted down like a wild beast? Roach must have wondered how something that seemed so great had turned into something so deadly. Gangs are not cave crews. Members don't join together to roast bear meat. When street gangs form, people die.

That brings me to the second question asked by Roach's mother: Why had someone hurt her son? Look at it this way. You're probably a different person when you're alone than when you're with others. Maybe you're quieter and you walk differently. But add one or two more people and things start happening, whether good or bad. There's more noise and (activity.) Sometimes you find that there are lots of things you might do when you're part of a crowd that you know you wouldn't do on your own. Things can get out of control—with people doing

◀ I think these questions are a clue to the middle of the speech. She's telling us what she is going to be talking about.

◀ Yes, the story was the introduction, and now I'm into the body of the speech.

◀ The speaker is answering the first question she asked by starting with history.

ESL/LEP: Have students define the words they selected before they suggest synonyms and antonyms for them.

Meeting Individual Needs: Help students see that this paragraph continues to answer the first organizing question.

◀ The speaker relates the idea of belonging back to Roach and what probably made him want to be in a gang.

Response Clue: Students should not confuse the writer's use of a question here with the questions she uses to organize the speech.

◀ Now the speaker is answering the second question. It helps to know what she is going to be talking about.

As you read, write notes in the margins about the structure of the speech.

something as (crazy) as hunting another boy down and killing him.

The boys who chased Roach that day didn't get arrested. Not that day anyway. A few of them grew up, but only a few. Most of them were dead before they were 18, and the others went to prison for one crime or another. I'm sure that, just like Roach, they loved belonging to their gang family. I'm also sure that as much as they loved (belonging,) they hated dying. Because when you die, no matter how many members of your gang show up at your funeral in their matching clothes, you die alone.

That brings us to the third question: What could Roach have done differently? We've already discussed how needing to belong is perfectly human and how joining a gang almost surely leads to death or crime. So where does that leave you?

Suppose, just (suppose,) that you took that same need that all of us have to belong and be respected—and chose life instead of death. How do you do that? It starts with the courage required to be an individual. While this is not easy, it's a lot easier than dying.

Roach, for instance, was a wonderful writer. Suppose he had taken pride in that (ability) and worked at it. Suppose he'd done something as strange as carrying a small notebook around with him so he could write down his thoughts and use them later in his stories. Suppose he'd gotten a babysitting job and saved money for college.

All that's a dream, of course. Roach didn't do any of that. But I did. And although I was every bit as lonely as Roach and wanted to belong, I wanted even more to live.

I have a family of my own today, and I'm proud to say I've written three books. That could not have happened had I joined the girl gang in our neighborhood. Now, when I think of Roach, and picture him running toward his death, I can only feel (grateful) that the road I chose—though lonely at first—was one that led me toward life. I hope you will choose that road, too.

Response Clue: Encourage students to continue looking for repeated words and to find synonyms for them.

Response Clue: Students should note that the speaker now addresses the third question.

Response Clue: Students might note that as the writer answers the third question and brings the subject back to herself, she is beginning her conclusion.

If you are working on

Lesson 9	Lesson 10
⬇	⬇
page 72	page 75

Clifford E. Trafzer directs the Native American Studies program at the University of California in Riverside. A Navajo, Trafzer often helps Native Americans put their ideas and stories into words. In writing this speech, Trafzer shares a message about the sacredness of land that is a common belief among many Native American cultures.

Preteaching Vocabulary: You may wish to preteach the following vocabulary words: *represent, proposal, lava, avalanche, sacred.*

Motivating Question: As they read, ask students to compare their views about nature with those of the speaker.

Our Lands Are Sacred

by Clifford E. Trafzer

As you read, write your own ideas about the structure of this speech. Make notes about the beginning, middle, and end of the speech.

I come here today to represent my people, who have given me many words to share with you. The most important thing they asked me to tell you is that the mountain is sacred to us. We do not want you to build a ski run with a lodge and condominiums on it. We believe the proposal to build on the mountain goes against our rights. I ask you to listen to my words. Listen to the story of the mountain and what it has been through. I ask that you listen with all your heart and mind. Perhaps you will be led to reconsider your proposal.

Response Clue: This beginning clearly introduces the topic. Students should also note the purpose of the speech.

We believe that the mountain was created when the earth was very young. In our old stories we learn that the sun created the mountain because the sun was lonely. He wanted the mountain to be close to him, a thing of beauty that he could admire. The sun created the base of the mountain out of the earth all around here. But the mountain was not tall enough for the sun, and so he heated up the inside of the earth and forced lava to flow out of the top of the mountain. The lava flowed for a long, long time, making the mountain tall and beautiful. The sun so loved the mountain that he sent his first light of morning to shine on its eastern side. Some of the elders say that the sun married the mountain.

Response Clue: The words circled here might inspire students to find synonyms and antonyms.

At the same time that the sun created the mountain, he placed a pipe inside the top of the peak. The pipe sends out peace and goodwill to the world. We believe that the pipe still lives inside the mountain. Only special people are allowed to go up on the sides of the mountain and that is why few of us go there. Still, we admire the mountain from far away, and we treasure it as our most precious gift. It is like a church to us.

ESL/LEP: Ask students who are having trouble coming up with synonyms and antonyms to demonstrate the meaning of *created, admire,* and *allowed* before finding synonyms and antonyms for these words. These words are easily demonstrated and have many synonyms and antonyms.

Many years ago the United States took the mountain from us. The U.S. Forest Service said that the mountain belonged to all of the people, not just Native Americans.

Response Clue: Students might note that the speaker is well into the body of the speech because he is supporting his topic with facts.

Response Clue: Students might write synonyms and antonyms for the words circled here.

Summarizing: Ask students to summarize the speaker's points in the body, or middle, of his speech.

Response Clue: Students should note that the speech is concluding. A summary of the main points ends the speech.

Cultural Awareness: Ask students to discuss how Native Americans feel about the mountain, the land, and nature in general.

The Forest Service allowed lumber companies to cut down the trees and sell the timber. We were opposed to cutting the trees because it scarred the face of the mountain. No one listened to our voices. The Forest Service and the lumber companies continued to log the mountain, and no one planted the trees to replace the ones that were cut.

In 1957 the Starland Development Company proposed to build a ski resort on the mountain. The Forest Service allowed the company to build it without consulting our people. My own father led a group of people to talk with the superintendent of the forest district. My father even warned the superintendent that it was dangerous to build on the side of the mountain. My father was remembering the old stories that say the sun and the mountain will destroy anything unnatural that is placed on the side of the mountain. Still, the superintendent did not listen.

In 1959, after the ski lodge had opened, an avalanche destroyed the ski lodge and killed 44 men, women, and children. The Forest Service transferred the superintendent, and we believe he was moved because he did not listen to our warning. All of this happened more than 30 years ago, but it is just like yesterday to my people. Imagine our surprise when we learned that you plan to build another ski lodge on the side of the mountain!

I am grateful that this time the Forest Service has talked to our people. This is a change and a good one, I think. You have also invited me to speak to you directly. This is another positive change.

Like my father before me, I represent my people. We feel strongly that you should not build on the mountain. We have a unique relationship with the mountain and we ask you to remember this. Do not build anything on the slopes of our mountain, the beautiful creation of the sun. Leave the mountain alone, to be enjoyed as the creator originally made it. Remember, the mountain is sacred.

Thank you.

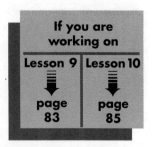

If you are working on

Lesson 9	Lesson 10
⬇	⬇
page 83	page 85

Reviewing *Structure of Speeches*

A. Read the speech "Our Lands Are Sacred" on pages 81-82. As you read, use the wide margins to make notes about the beginning, middle, and end of the speech. Then use your own words to fill in the chart below.

Reviewing the Strategy: Have students use the sidenotes they wrote on pages 81-82 to help them determine the speech's beginning, middle, and end.

Managing the Lesson: Answers on the chart are suggestions.

Beginning

- **What is the topic of the speech?**

A resort should not be built.

- **Does it inform by giving facts?**
- **Does it try to persuade you to think or act in some way?**
- **Does it inspire you?**

The purpose is persuasive: to reconsider building the resort.

Middle

- **What details does the writer give to support the topic?**

Students may mention that the land is sacred or that an avalanche wiped out the earlier resort.

End

- **Describe the ending of the speech. Does it summarize the ideas stated in the rest of the speech? Does it restate the topic?**

The speaker summarizes and restates his appeal.

B. How did Clifford Trafzer organize his information in the beginning, middle, and end of his speech? Use details from the chart above to support your conclusions.

Students should use the information on their chart to help them organize their work. They may mention that in the first paragraph, Trafzer states the topic of the speech— that a ski resort should not be built—and makes it clear that his purpose is to persuade others not to build the resort. In the middle of the speech, Trafzer supports this topic by clarifying that the land is sacred and that an avalanche wiped out an earlier resort. Finally, Trafzer restates the topic and summarizes his appeal.

Cooperative Learning: If students have trouble relating their notes to the graphic, have them work in groups of three to complete the chart.

| Lesson 9 | Introducing page 72 | Practicing page 73 | Applying page 74 | Reviewing page 83 | Testing page 84 |

Testing *Structure of Speeches*

A. Each pair of sentences contains only one statement that is true. Circle the true statement in each pair. Explain your answer on the line that follows.

1. (a.) The beginning of "Our Lands Are Sacred" explains the purpose of the speech.

 b. The beginning of "Our Lands Are Sacred" explains that the Native Americans have no hope of saving the mountain.

The speaker introduces the topic and why he is speaking.

2. a. In the middle of the speech, the speaker explains that because the moon was lonely, it wanted the mountain.

 (b.) In the middle of the speech, the speaker explains his beliefs about the origin of the mountain.

The speaker supports his topic by explaining why the mountain is sacred.

3. (a.) In the middle of the speech, Clifford Trafzer also tells the history of an earlier attempt to build a ski lodge on the mountain.

 b. In the middle of the speech, Clifford Trafzer also says that this is the first attempt to build on the sacred mountain.

This detail supports the topic of the speech.

4. a. In the ending of the speech, the speaker suggests the Forest Service build only a small park on the mountain.

 (b.) In the end of the speech, the speaker asks the Forest Service not to build a ski resort on sacred land.

The speaker restates his appeal to keep the mountain in its natural state.

B. Imagine you can vote on whether or not to allow the ski resort and condos to be built. How will you vote? Why? Tell how the speech influenced your opinion.

Responses will differ, but students should mention details from the speech that

influenced them. Their writing should state its purpose in the beginning, support that

purpose with details, and conclude with a summary or restatement of the topic.

To begin
Lesson 10

page
75

Lesson 10	Introducing page 75	Practicing page 76	Applying page 77	Reviewing page 85	Testing page 86

Reviewing Synonyms and Antonyms

A. Reread "Our Lands Are Sacred" on pages 81-82, circling any words for which you know synonyms and antonyms. Choose one of these words, and use it to complete the diagram below.

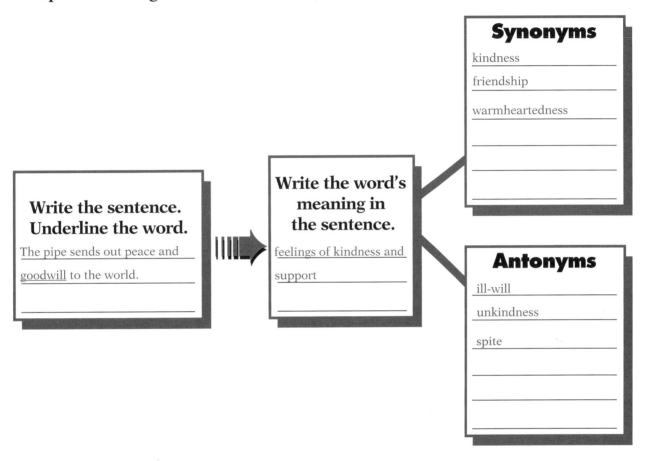

Write the sentence. Underline the word.

The pipe sends out peace and goodwill to the world.

Write the word's meaning in the sentence.

feelings of kindness and support

Synonyms

kindness

friendship

warmheartedness

Antonyms

ill-will

unkindness

spite

B. Choose a topic you know people disagree about, such as a music group, a type of music, or a sports team. List two negative and two positive words to describe your topic. Then list two synonyms and two antonyms for each word on your list. Explain how they are different from the words you chose first to describe your topic.

Responses will vary. Encourage students to use a dictionary as they work. If they use

a thesaurus, suggest that they check the meanings of these words in a dictionary.

Reviewing the Strategy: Have students refer to words they circled in the selection. Remind students to use a dictionary to check the meanings of the words they choose.

Managing the Lesson: Answers on the diagram are suggestions. Students may choose other synonyms and antonyms.

Cooperative Learning: Have students complete Section B orally, in small groups, with one recorder writing each group's responses.

Assessing Cooperative Work: Note the degree to which group members listen to each other, contribute to the discussion, and add relevant information.

Unit 5 Lesson 10 ■ **85**

Test-Taking Hints:
Encourage students to
pace themselves on
timed tests and to be
sure to mark the items
in the way specified, in
this case by checking
the correct box.

Testing Synonyms and Antonyms

A. Read each pair of sentences below. Check the box labeled "S" if the underlined words are *synonyms*. Check the box labeled "A" if the underlined words are *antonyms*. Then explain your answer on the line that follows.

1. Letitia and Fran are <u>strong</u> skaters.

Letitia and Fran are <u>powerful</u> skaters.

S [✓]

A [ ]

Both words mean "having physical force."

2. The air deep between city buildings was <u>freezing</u>.

The air deep between city buildings was <u>scorching</u>.

S [ ]

A [✓]

These words describe opposite temperature ranges.

ESL/LEP: You may
wish to clarify the
meanings of the
underlined words with
students before they
answer the questions in
Section A.

3. I'm sorry Aunt Agatha was so <u>sharp</u> when she phoned.

I'm sorry Aunt Agatha sounded so <u>impatient</u> when she phoned.

S [✓]

A [ ]

Both words mean "harsh and gruff."

4. Juana was very <u>bossy</u> this morning.

Juana was very <u>cooperative</u> this morning.

S [ ]

A [✓]

These words describe quite different behaviors.

Assessing Student
Writing: Rate student
writing on a scale of 1-
4, with 1 being the least
degree and 4 being the
greatest degree. Use the
following criteria: uses
a topic sentence, uses
supporting details,
develops ideas
logically, and uses a
closing sentence.

B. Write a descriptive paragraph about something you like very much, such as a car, a sport, or a television program. Then underline five positive words you have used. In the margin, write a synonym or an antonym and label it "S" or "A."

Student should draw a clear picture of a favorite object or TV program. Responses

should indicate their understanding of the difference between synonyms and

antonyms. They should underline five words they have used and write a synonym or

antonym for each in the margins.

Unit SIX

BECOMING AN ACTIVE READER

Good readers are critical readers. When they read a **speech**, good readers think about what they already know and compare it to what they read. Good readers use this knowledge to help them understand a writer's message.

Using Skills and Strategies

Asking questions about persuasive language will help you find the **author's purpose** in speeches you read. You may ask: How does the author appeal to my feelings? What reasons does the author use to back up the topic? What is the author trying to persuade me to think or do?

Making judgments about the facts and opinions presented is another strategy that good readers use. You may ask: Where are the facts? Where are the opinions? Do these facts and opinions agree with what I already know? Does this speech convince me to act or think in a new way?

In this unit, finding the **author's purpose** and **making judgments** will help you read more critically.

The Speech: The Writer's Voice

Spoken language is far older than written language. All civilizations have been shaped by the facts and opinions presented in speeches. As you read a persuasive speech, imagine that you are hearing the writer make the speech. Think about your reactions to what is being said and what the writer is trying to convince you to think or do. You will be following an old, old tradition.

Responding to Speeches

Good readers respond to the persuasive language and facts and opinions presented in speeches. You may find yourself agreeing or disagreeing with the writer of " 'No' To Drugs, 'Yes' To Your Future" and "Your Education Is Your Future." Jot down these thoughts in the side margins as you read. Writing sidenotes will help you think about your reactions to the speech. Refer to them as you discuss the speech with your classmates.

Unit Enrichment: Students might enjoy reading the speeches aloud. You might even encourage individuals to select sections of each speech to present to the class. Students might enjoy augmenting their presentation with charts, illustrations, or additional anecdotes.

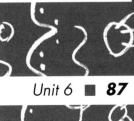

Author's Purpose

Lesson Objective: To identify the author's purpose by analyzing facts and opinions in the speeches " 'No' to Drugs, 'Yes' to Your Future" and "Your Education Is Your Future."

ESL/LEP: Model using persuasive language, gestures, and facial expressions to convince a student that one sport is better than another.

Modeling the Strategy: Read aloud a passage from a magazine article to model author's purpose. Refer to the steps in the chart. After completing the page, use the Reproducible Activity Master on page T15 of the ATE to help students apply the strategy to " 'No' to Drugs, 'Yes' to Your Future."

Managing the Lesson: Remind students to use the sidenotes on pages 94-95 to model the process of active reading and to help them answer questions 1 and 2.

Introducing Strategies

In persuasive speeches, the **author's purpose** is to convince the audience to think or act in a particular way. The writer usually states the main point clearly and gives opinions, facts, and examples to support it.

Throughout the speech, a writer may use persuasive language to appeal to a reader's feelings or make a clear, powerful appeal to reason. Good readers look for persuasive language as a key to the author's purpose.

The chart that follows shows a strategy for determining the purpose of a persuasive speech.

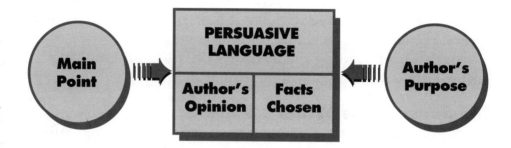

Reading the Speech

Read " 'No' to Drugs, 'Yes' to Your Future" and the sidenotes on pages 94-95. These notes show how one good reader looked for the author's purpose in this persuasive speech. Use the sidenotes to answer the questions below.

1. What does the reader think Sager wants you to think or do?

The reader thinks Sager wants students to decide for themselves to stay healthy and

to avoid abusing drugs.

2. List two examples of persuasive language that the reader has found.

The phrase "going nowhere fast" appeals to the reader's feeling of fear; "break her

heart" appeals to the reader's feelings and concerns.

Practicing *Author's Purpose*

A. Circle the item that completes each statement most persuasively. Explain your choice on the line that follows it.

1. Carol Sager says that the Energizer rabbit
   (a.) is going nowhere—fast.
   b. knows what he's doing.
   c. knows where he's going.
   d. is going in circles.
   Sager uses a well-known phrase for emphasis.

2. Carol Sager says that to see any one of the students end up going nowhere
   a. would make her sad.
   (b) would break her heart.
   c. would stop her from feeling proud.
   d. would be bad for the students.
   This phrase is the strongest statement of the four.

3. Carol Sager says that young people "want to be able to walk down the street and not be afraid that some drugged or drunken driver will . . . ."
   (a) run up on the sidewalk and crush them.
   b. hurt them.
   c. run over them.
   d. run into them.
   This phrase draws a vivid picture of the dangers of drug or alcohol use.

B. Think of one idea that would make the world a better place. Write a brief speech in which you use persuasive language to convince your audience to accept your idea. After you write your speech, add one sentence that states your purpose.

Encourage students to choose topics about which they have strong feelings. Examples

of persuasive language should appeal to the emotions of the reader and reflect the

feelings of the writer. Check to see that each student's statement of purpose is

supported by the ideas in his or her speech.

Purpose: The purpose of this page is to help students determine the author's purpose in a speech. Questions reflect the strategy illustrated on the **Introducing** page.

Peer Sharing: Have students complete Section A independently, then work with a partner to compare answers. Encourage students to make sure their partners provide details from the speech to support their responses.

Writing Process: Students might choose to develop their responses into full-length speeches as a total writing process activity.

Applying Author's Purpose

Applying the Skill to Other Media: Invite students to identify persuasive language that they have read or heard in speeches and interviews in newspapers or on TV. Have students tell how this language affects them as readers or listeners.

A. Read the speech below, which was given by a candidate for class representative in a student government election. Then answer the questions that follow it.

Why am I a candidate? The other night on television, I heard a speech given by a national politician to a student audience. This politician explained how years before, when she was a member of her school government, she had learned to speak up for what she believed in. She liked helping others by acting as their spokeswoman and representative. I, too, want to help others. I also want to express my concerns for problems that affect our school. I can help start new programs for our school.

I want to found a "We Love Seniors" student group, for students to share energy, time, and love with retired people. We can leap forward in our learning if we spend time with them. That's why I am running. That's why I am asking for your vote.

ESL/LEP: Make sure students understand that *Seniors* in this context refers to older people.

Individualized Learning: Have students complete the page independently. Make sure their responses correctly reflect details in the passage.

1. What is the author's purpose in this speech?

The author wants the readers or listeners to vote for her.

2. List some examples of persuasive language she used.

Students may suggest quotes that help persuade the reader to vote for the speaker, such as "I, too, want to help others" and "I can help start new programs for our school."

Cooperative Learning: Have students work in groups of three or four to revise the speech to make it more persuasive. Groups might present their speech to the class.

B. Do you think the reference to the woman who is now in national government helps the writer persuade the audience? Explain how you might make the speech more persuasive.

The speaker suggests that he or she is similar to the woman in national government. Students should suggest that the speech can be made more persuasive by supporting an issue that more closely affects the students, such as raising funds for a swimming pool. The speaker might also appeal to the emotions of the audience by playing on their fears, saying that she will make the campus safe.

To review

↓

page 99

Making Judgments

| Lesson 12 | Introducing page 91 | Practicing page 92 | Practicing page 93 | Practicing page 101 | Practicing page 102 |

Introducing Strategies

In persuasive speeches, writers include both facts and opinions. Facts can be proved; opinions must be supported by facts or examples. In judging a persuasive speech, good readers first determine which points are facts and which are opinions. Then they check to see if the facts and opinions agree with what they already know. Next, they check to see if the facts and opinions fit with their own values and attitudes. Finally, readers **make a judgment** about the speech. They may then choose whether or not to think or act as the speech suggests.

The chart that follows shows a strategy for judging persuasive speeches.

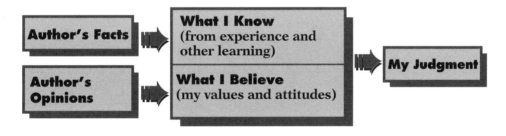

Reading the Speech

Reread " 'No' to Drugs, 'Yes' to Your Future" on pages 94-95. Circle the facts that you find and underline the opinions. Then answer the questions below.

1. Give one fact and one opinion that you found.

Facts may include: "Drugs can kill—even the first time you use them." Opinions may

include: "the Energizer rabbit is going nowhere—fast."

2. How do your experiences and beliefs help you make a judgment about the speech?

Students should mention movies, TV programs, or experiences that influence their

judgment.

Lesson Objective: To make judgments by analyzing facts and opinions in the speeches " 'No' to Drugs, 'Yes' to Your Future" and "Your Education Is Your Future."

ESL/LEP: Review the definition of *facts* and *opinions*. Then have students give examples of each one.

Modeling the Strategy: Read aloud a passage from a newspaper to model making judgments. Refer to the steps in the chart. After completing the page, use the Reproducible Activity Master on page T13 of the ATE to help students apply the strategy to " 'No' to Drugs, 'Yes' to Your Future."

Managing the Lesson: Tell students that noting facts and opinions helps them become active readers. Remind them that their notes will help them answer questions 1 and 2.

Practicing Making Judgments

A. Circle the letter in front of the best answer for each question. Then, on the line that follows, explain your choice.

1. Which of the following is one of the author's opinions?
    a. Some people who try drugs end up in wheelchairs, or worse.
    b. Young people believe that using drugs, tobacco, or alcohol is not cool.
    c. Drug use is costing our country billions of dollars.
    (d.) Students tell her they won't drink because drinking makes people look silly.

This statement cannot be supported by facts or studies.

2. Which of the following statements from the essay do you believe is a reasonable opinion?
    a. It helps when adults tell young people what to do.
    b. Most people don't and won't use drugs.
    c. Everyone looks down on smokers.
    (d.) Young people want to feel safe.

The other statements could be debated.

3. Based on your experience, values, and attitudes, which one of the following judgments about the speech is correct?
    (a.) The speaker's facts were true: her opinions were believable. She made her point well.
    b. The speaker's facts were all wrong, so her opinions don't matter.
    c. I don't believe the speaker's facts or agree with her opinions, but I'll follow her advice.
    d. The speaker doesn't try to persuade you to do or think anything in particular.

The speaker uses facts and reasonable opinions to persuade students to make healthy choices.

B. Which one of the author's opinions do you agree with most? Explain your ideas using support from your own experience as well as your values and attitudes.

Students should cite an opinion in the speech with which they agree and support their

choice with their experiences, values, and attitudes.

Purpose: The purpose of this page is to help students make judgments on the information presented in a speech. Questions reflect the strategy of relating facts and opinions to the reader's attitudes and beliefs illustrated on the **Introducing** page.

Individualized Learning: Have students complete the page independently. Make sure that their explanations for Section A support the items they have chosen.

Conferencing: Have students work with a peer to identify the details, attitudes, and personal experiences that support their responses.

Applying *Making Judgments*

A. Read this short persuasive speech. Then answer the questions that follow it.

You might think that writing well is only important if your goal in life is to become a famous writer. Writing, however, is a form of communication, and you need good communication skills to succeed no matter what your goals are. Good writers can share deep feelings in letters to people they care about. They can influence the opinions of others about an important community problem in letters to newspaper editors. Think of the pleasure you could give a younger student if you wrote and illustrated a children's book. Then think of the argument you could present to a future employer that would result in a salary raise. Do you still think writing well is unimportant?

1. What is this speech trying to persuade you to think or do?

The speech tries to show readers the importance of good writing skills and to

persuade them to improve their own writing skills.

2. According to the speech, what happens when you are able to communicate in writing?

Students may suggest that good writing skills help a person influence public opinion,

give pleasure to others, and attain goals.

B. What judgment did you make about the topic after reading this speech? Support your answer with your own knowledge, experience, and attitudes.

Students should explain a judgment they made about the speech and support their

response with their knowledge, experiences, and attitudes.

Applying the Skill to Everyday Reading: Students can practice making judgments and analyzing facts and opinions in editorials they read in local or school newspapers. Encourage students to share editorials that interest them and discuss how they made judgments about the facts and opinions presented.

Cooperative Learning: Have students complete Section A in groups of three. One student should be the reader, another the moderator, and the third the recorder. Students need not reach a consensus, but should be able to support their responses.

Individualized Learning: Have students underline the experiences and attitudes that support their judgment.

To review
page 101

The title tells the author's opinion about what students should do if drugs are offered to them. I wonder if the author will explain why she feels this way. What will she say to convince me of this opinion?

The notes in the margin show how one reader analyzed the author's purpose in this speech.

Most teenagers will know this TV commercial. Bringing up something familiar catches my attention.

I agree with the author about "going no place fast." The thought scares me. This appeals to my feeling of fear—she's using persuasive language.

She says she cares very much and that it would "break her heart" if I went nowhere fast. She's appealing to my feelings to make her point.

Motivating Question: As students read, ask them what the author wants young people to do.

She's using persuasive language to tell us her credentials—a good appeal to reason.

Response Clue: The circled facts and underlined opinions are a few examples that students might identify as they read.

Some of the persuasive language here appeals to reason—an expert giving facts to back up her opinion. I bet Sager wants us to make our own decisions, but she's trying to persuade us that drugs are not a good choice.

Carol Sager is a respected substance-abuse prevention specialist and author. As a national consultant, she helped develop the National Drug-Free School Recognition Program. Perhaps some day you'll be fortunate enough to hear Dr. Sager speak in person. In the speech that follows, Dr. Sager encourages young people to take care of themselves and make healthy choices for the future.

"No" to Drugs, "Yes" to Your Future

by Carol Sager

How many of you are familiar with the Energizer rabbit—the one that keeps going, on and on and on? How many of you know where that rabbit is going?

Everybody knows about the rabbit. Everybody knows what he does. Nobody knows where he's going. In other words, the Energizer rabbit is going nowhere—fast.

And the same can be said about anyone who gets involved in using tobacco, alcohol, or other drugs. Sooner or later, users end up like the Energizer rabbit—going round and round in circles—going no place fast.

I decided not to tell you to say "No" to using tobacco, alcohol, and other drugs. It's not that I don't care whether or not you use drugs. I do care very much. It would break my heart to see any one of you end up like the Energizer rabbit—going no place fast.

I've been in the drug-use prevention business for a long time. I have seen too many young people—just like you—end up in wheelchairs or worse because they said "OK" when a classmate asked them to try some dope. Drugs can kill—even the first time you use them.

Yes, I do care. So why am I not going to spend the morning telling you to say "No" to drugs? I have two reasons. First, when I was your age, it seemed that all adults ever did was tell me what not to do. Don't chew with your mouth open, don't throw your clean clothes on the floor, don't wipe your nose on your sleeve— don't, don't, don't. After a while, I would stop listening every time an adult used the word don't. So I won't say don't. You'd only tune me out when I talked.

The second reason I won't say don't is that most of you will say it yourself. That's right—most young people don't and won't use drugs. As part of my business, I talk with a lot of young people all over the country. Most of them know that using illegal drugs or using legal drugs in ways other than what a doctor prescribes is against the law and harmful to their health. They also know that drug use is costing the country billions and billions of dollars. They know that this money could be used to find homes for the homeless, discover a cure for cancer, or make sure no one had to worry about having enough food to eat. Young people, like everyone else, want to live in a safe environment. They want to be able to walk down the street and not be afraid that some drugged or drunken driver will run up on the sidewalk and crush them. They want to come to school and not be afraid of gangs and violence. They know that the increases in crime, violence, and fatal accidents are all directly related to drug use.

Most importantly, most young people know that using tobacco, alcohol, or other drugs is not cool. Wherever I go, I hear the same comments. Kids tell me, "I am not going to smoke because I don't want to stink. Besides, everyone looks down on smokers." Or they say, "I'm not going to drink because alcohol makes people act silly." And "Cocaine? No way! That stuff kills you!"

So instead of telling you what to say "No" to, I want to talk about what I hope you will say "Yes" to. As I look out at all of you sitting here at this assembly, I see the future senators, future writers, future engineers, and future scientists of this country. I know that among you are all the talents and skills needed to make this a better world, to build lasting peace, and to ease pain and suffering. I also know that you are my future. Someday, I am going to have to depend on you to take care of me.

The thing I want you to do for me and mostly for yourselves is—stay healthy! Eat nourishing foods. Get plenty of rest. Exercise your body. Avoid harmful behaviors. Be sure to exercise your mind, too. Set challenging goals for yourselves. Whatever you choose to do, give it your all. The world doesn't need a bunch of Energizer rabbits, going no place fast.

In conclusion, someone once defined "horse sense" as the good sense horses have not to bet on people. But you and I have no choice. We have to bet on people for our future. And, when we bet on people, it's good to know that there are clear-headed, healthy people like you around. As I look at you, I have faith in the future because I have faith in you.

You will stay healthy. You will say "Yes" to your future.

As you read, write your own notes in the margins about how persuasive language helps you understand the purpose of this speech.

Additional Skills: This selection may also be used to teach recognizing the structure of speeches (see ATE page 72) and identifying cause and effect (see ATE page 59).

Response Clue: This paragraph includes facts and opinions that reflect the author's purpose. Discuss or check students' reactions to them.

Summarizing: Have students discuss the choices to which Sager hopes that students will say "No" or "Yes."

Clarification: You may wish to have students reread this paragraph to clarify what the author means by healthy and harmful behaviors.

If you are working on

Lesson 11	Lesson 12
page 88	page 91

Frank Sifuentes understands firsthand the importance of an education. As a teen, he dropped out of school only to find his life was going nowhere. Eventually, Sifuentes went back to school and earned a college degree from UCLA. Today he runs a successful communication business and enjoys helping young Latino writers to publish their works. As the following speech illustrates, Sifuentes wants to keep students from making the same mistake he did.

Your Education Is Your Future

by Frank Moreno Sifuentes

I speak to you today in what I believe is the most important place to you—school. Why is this place so important? Because here you are preparing for your future. If you care about that preparation—about your education—your future will be bright. I guarantee it. If you turn your back on education, I have no guarantees—-except one. If you leave school, I guarantee your future will include regret.

I know this because I have experienced it myself. In eighth grade, I began going to a new school. It was a huge school, and there were very few Latino students. Often, I felt left out. Every time something little didn't go right for me, I felt discouraged. Finally, I gave up. I begged my mother to let me quit school and go to work. She agreed, and I thought, "I'm free!" However, within a year I knew what a terrible mistake I had made. I had nothing in common with other kids my age. More importantly, I had no future.

I went back to school determined to succeed. I knew I was working for my life, for my future. I became a good student who earned scholarships and went on to college. My decision to go back to school was the best I've ever made.

I want you to make good decisions, too. Start today. Decide to be the best you can be. How can you make that decision a reality? By staying in school. Education is a key—to jobs, to power, to money, to enriching the lives of others. By staying in school, you decide to meet life's challenges.

"Wait a minute!" some of you might be saying. You might be thinking that everyone does not have an equal chance, that you don't all start out with the same benefits.

It's true that some of you started out with better opportunities than others. Some of you might get more attention than others. But these differences are all washed away when you do one simple thing—believe in yourself. When you believe in yourself, you give yourself a chance. When you believe in yourself, you give yourself encouragement to succeed.

I can see that some of you still look doubtful. Perhaps you've heard about people who "made it big" at a young age, without an education. But those stories only tell some of the truth. They don't tell what happens to those same people five or ten years later, after their talents or lucky streaks have worn out. They don't tell what happens to those people when they discover that their inability to read or write well stops them from moving ahead. They don't tell about the regret these people feel, wishing they'd stayed in school.

Additional Skills: This selection may also be used to teach identifying author's viewpoint (see ATE page 39).

ESL/LEP: Distinguish between the literal and figurative meanings of the idioms *made it big* and *lucky streaks*.

Response Clue: Students may note that the author's purpose—to convince students to stay in school—is clear in this paragraph.

Meeting Individual Needs: Reluctant readers tend to read, or become involved in reading, as little as possible. Ask these students to circle one fact and underline one opinion (examples are marked in the ATE on pages 96-98). Then encourage them to make a judgment based on the fact and opinion they find.

I can give you an example that includes the whole story. How many of you have heard of Fernando Valenzuela? He was one of the greatest pitchers the Los Angeles Dodgers ever had.

Fernando Valenzuela grew up in poverty in Sonora, Mexico. He wanted "out." He decided the only way he could get "out" was to become a great baseball player. So, he spent all of his time playing baseball. He forgot about school, about anything but the sport he believed would save him.

Now, I'm not cutting down Valenzuela's dedication to his goal. What I am suggesting is that he was very short-sighted about the future.

You see, when Fernando Valenzuela made it big in baseball, he found out he had not made it big in life. In his new community, he did not know the language or the culture. He did not have basic survival skills that an education could have given him. Valenzuela began feeling bad about himself. In a country that values education above all, he had none.

At this point Fernando made a very smart decision. He decided to go to school. He dedicated himself to learning English. Was it hard? Yes, probably the hardest thing he'll ever do. Was it worth it? You decide. Today Fernando Valenzuela doesn't feel bad about himself at all. And he often talks to young people about getting an education.

Like Fernando Valenzuela, I don't want to see young people going through dark moments of regret. I want you to feel good about yourselves. I want you to stay in school. But the decision is yours.

If you are working on

Lesson 11	Lesson 12
↓	↓
page 99	page 101

Reviewing *Author's Purpose*

A. Read "Your Education Is Your Future" on pages 96-98. Use the wide margins to take notes about the author's purpose for writing the speech. To help you organize your ideas, complete the chart below.

Reviewing the Strategy: Have students refer to the sidenotes they wrote on pages 96-98. Tell them to complete the chart, writing opinions, facts, persuasive language, the main point, and the author's purpose on the lines provided.

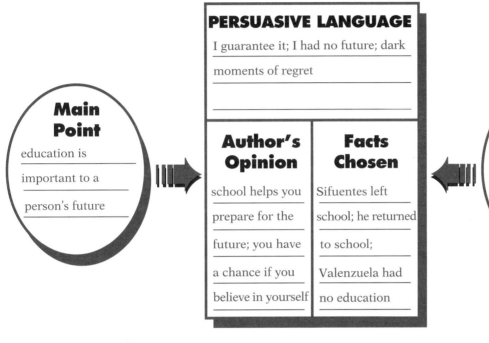

Main Point

education is

important to a

person's future

PERSUASIVE LANGUAGE

I guarantee it; I had no future; dark

moments of regret

_____

Author's Opinion

school helps you

prepare for the

future; you have

a chance if you

believe in yourself

Facts Chosen

Sifuentes left

school; he returned

to school;

Valenzuela had

no education

Author's Purpose

to convince students

to stay in school

and study hard

Managing the Lesson: Answers on the chart are suggestions. Students may cite other examples from the selection.

Cooperative Learning: Have students work in groups of three to write and present the new topic.

B. How do you think Sifuentes's speech might be different if its title were "Sports Are Your Future"? Write a paragraph that expresses this opinion. Make sure you include persuasive language, facts, and opinions that support this new purpose.

Students should state the revised purpose of the speech in their first sentence, then

offer persuasive language, facts, and opinions to explain why "sports are their future."

_____

_____

_____

_____

_____

_____

_____

Test-Taking Hints:
Tell students that when they take reading tests they may have to choose the true statement among a number of alternatives. They should keep in mind the strategy for identifying author's purpose as they make their decisions. Point out that time on a test is limited, therefore, students should not spend too much time on any one item.

Meeting Individual Needs: Students who have found this speech challenging may need to review the author's opinions and the facts that support them.

Assessing Student Writing: Rate student writing on a scale of 1-4, with 1 being the least degree and 4 being the greatest degree. Use the following criteria: originality, organization, reasoning, and clarity.

To begin Lesson 12

page 91

Lesson 11	Introducing page 88	Practicing page 89	Applying page 90	Reviewing page 99	Testing page 100

Testing Author's Purpose

A. Read the statements below and fill in the bubble next to each true statement. On the lines that follow, explain your response.

● **1.** The author feels that school is an important factor in determining the quality of a person's future.

The author states that education prepares people for the future.

○ **2.** The author uses an example from his own life to show that it's easy to be successful without an education.

The author points out what a terrible mistake he made by leaving school.

○ **3.** The author believes that anybody with a very great talent can succeed and be happy throughout life even without an education.

The author tells how the famous pitcher Fernando Valenzuela did not have basic

survival skills without an education.

○ **4.** The author thinks that young people should be forced to stay in school.

The author says that this is a decision the students must make for themselves.

● **5.** The author's purpose is to persuade students to stay in school.

The author tries to persuade students that staying in school will help them to have a

better future.

B. Think of an issue that you feel strongly about. Then write a paragraph to persuade other students to agree with you. Use persuasive language and be sure to choose facts that support your opinions.

Students should state their position on an issue in their first sentence, then support it

with facts, opinions, and persuasive language.

Reviewing *Making Judgments*

A. Reread "Your Education Is Your Future" on pages 96-98. Circle the facts and underline the opinions that influenced the judgment you made about the speech. Then use the chart below to help you organize your ideas.

Reviewing the Strategy: Have students refer to the facts they circled and the opinions they underlined on pages 96-98. Tell them to use this information to help them make judgments about the speech.

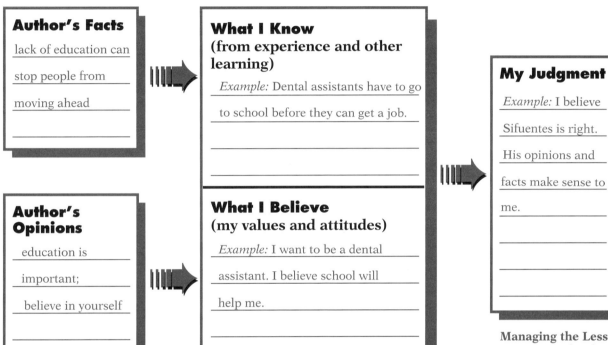

Author's Facts

lack of education can
stop people from
moving ahead

What I Know
(from experience and other learning)

Example: Dental assistants have to go
to school before they can get a job.

Author's Opinions

education is
important;
believe in yourself

What I Believe
(my values and attitudes)

Example: I want to be a dental
assistant. I believe school will
help me.

My Judgment

Example: I believe
Sifuentes is right.
His opinions and
facts make sense to
me.

B. In what ways do you think the author's ideas were influenced by his experiences and attitudes?

Students may suggest that he may not have valued education so highly if he hadn't
quit school, then noticed that he had no future. Also, had he not returned to school,
he might not have known what he could achieve.

Managing the Lesson: Answers on the chart are suggestions. Students may cite other facts and opinions from the speech and draw on their own experiences and values.

Peer Sharing: Have students complete Section A independently, then work with a partner to compare answers.

Student Self-Assessment: Students might wish to evaluate their own writing on a scale of 1-4, with 1 being the least degree and 4 being the greatest degree. Have them use the following criteria: Did I answer the question? Did I use examples from the text? Are my ideas clearly stated?

Lesson 12	Introducing page 91	Practicing page 92	Applying page 93	Reviewing page 101	Testing page 102

Testing Making Judgments

A. Circle the item that best completes each statement below about "Your Education Is Your Future." Some statements may be completed with more than one phrase. Explain your answer on the line that follows.

1. What has the author learned from experience?
   a. Experience is the best educator.
   b. Self-esteem is not affected by education.
   c. Few U.S. citizens value education.
   ⓓ Education is the key to success and self-esteem.
   Education helps you meet life's challenges.

2. What are the author's values and attitudes?
   ⓐ He values education and believes everyone should go to school.
   b. He values success no matter how it is achieved.
   c. He believes school keeps teenagers out of trouble.
   d. He thinks that self-esteem is the key to success and happiness.
   He believes that success in life is almost impossible without an education.

3. What facts does the author use to support his opinions?
   a. Fernando Valenzuela succeeded in life despite his lack of education.
   ⓑ As teenagers, the author and Valenzuela did not value education.
   ⓒ The author and Valenzuela went back to school because they regretted dropping out.
   d. The author was a successful baseball player who had no education and little self-esteem.
   The author went back to school and became a success; Valenzuela gained self-respect.

B. After reading "Your Education Is Your Future," what judgment did you make about the topic? Explain your reasons.

Students should state their judgment and support this response with facts and

opinions from the speech and their own beliefs and experiences.

Unit SEVEN

BECOMING AN ACTIVE READER

Active readers are critical readers. They summarize the points a writer makes in an **essay**. Summarizing helps good readers keep the writer's ideas clear in their mind.

Using Skills and Strategies

Asking questions will help you become involved with the essays you read. You may ask: Is the author trying to entertain me? Has the author included personal information? If the answer to these questions is yes, you are probably reading an **informal essay**. Is the topic serious? Does the writer discuss ideas? If the answer to these questions is yes, you are probably reading a **formal essay**.

One way to get involved in an essay is to search for its **main idea**. You may ask: What is the most important point the author is making? What **details** support this point? Recognizing the main idea helps you focus on what the author is telling you.

In this unit, learning to identify **formal and informal essays** and to recognize **main ideas and details** will help you read essays actively.

The Essay: The Writer's Voice

Essays can break down cultural barriers by examining topics important to a person and a culture. Essays present ideas and details that help readers understand different points of view. Sometimes essays are humorous. These informal essays can also show a need for change. In helping us explore different ideas, essays can enlarge our world.

Responding to Essays

Good readers respond to essays by considering their ideas and deciding whether or not they agree with them. If the essay is effective, the reader may gain a new opinion based on the writer's ideas. Jot down your responses in the margins as you read "Why *Roots* Is an Important Work to African Americans" and "Advertising." Use these notes as you discuss the essays with your classmates.

Unit Enrichment: Invite students to collect essays from magazines and newspapers. Each student's collection should center on a personal interest, such as sports, entertainment, or an art form. You may wish to show the students several different ways to bind the essays into scrapbooks. For example, display papers in a three-ring binder, hole-punched and bound with yarn, and stitched with heavy thread.

Reading Essays

Introducing Strategies

An **essay** is a short nonfiction work on one subject. The purpose of an **informal essay** is to entertain. The writer may provide personal information about himself or herself in addition to information on the essay's subject. Informal essays often contain humor.

The purpose of a **formal essay** is to discuss a serious topic. The writer presents facts and discusses ideas. Formal essays rarely contain humor or personal information.

The checklist below can help you decide if an essay is informal or formal.

ESSAY CHECKLIST

Informal Essay
- [ ] informal tone (sounds as if the writer is chatting with the reader)
- [ ] the writer tells something about himself or herself
- [ ] may contain humor
- [ ] purpose is to entertain

Formal Essay
- [ ] serious tone, not humorous
- [ ] carefully organized, not rambling or chatty
- [ ] not much personal information
- [ ] purpose is to discuss a serious topic

Reading the Essay

Read "Why *Roots* Is an Important Work to African Americans" and the sidenotes on pages 110-111. The sidenotes show one good reader's thoughts about formal and informal essays. Use these notes to answer the questions below.

1. Does the reader think this essay is formal or informal?

The reader thinks this is a formal essay.

2. Give two reasons the reader found to support this opinion.

Students may include any two of the four reasons presented in the Formal Essay

section of the Essay Checklist.

Practicing Reading Essays

A. In each item below, circle the letter of the true statement. Then, on the lines that follow it, explain your choice.

1. a. The writer makes connections between his own childhood and Alex Haley's.
   (b) In "Why *Roots* Is an Important Work to African Americans," the writer makes connections between the cultures of Africans and African Americans.

   In this formal essay, the author does not speak about himself, but he does compare

   cultures.

2. a. In this essay, Donald E. Winbush tells amusing stories of his own boyhood in Africa.
   (b) In this essay, Donald E. Winbush talks seriously about the importance of understanding one's own culture.

   Winbush thinks that understanding culture is a serious topic, so he uses a formal

   tone.

3. (a.) This is a formal essay because it is on a serious topic and the writer speaks in a formal way.
   b. This is an informal essay because the writer tells about humorous events and sounds as if he were talking directly to me.

   This formal essay is serious in tone and style; it is not humorous.

B. Imagine that you are starting a project to look for your own roots. Decide if you will write in a formal or informal tone. Then describe at least two things you might do to get started.

Students should choose a tone—formal or informal—in which they will write. They

should also describe two things they would do in order to get started, for example:

interviewing their parents and grandparents, looking through old family albums and

books, obtaining old family letters (first getting permission to do so), obtaining copies

of legal records (such as birth certificates and marriage licenses).

Purpose: The purpose of this page is to help students practice the skill of comparing the characteristics of formal and informal essays. Questions reflect the strategy illustrated on the checklist on the **Introducing** page.

Individualized Learning: Have students complete the page independently. Make sure that their explanations for Section A support the items they circled.

Conferencing: Have students work with a peer to plan an essay and the details that might be included.

| Lesson 13 | Introducing page 104 | Practicing page 105 | Applying page 106 | Reviewing page 117 | Testing page 118 |

Applying Reading Essays

A. Read the excerpt from the essay "Snakes, Just Snakes" below. The writer of the essay is referring to a newspaper article reporting the story of a man who has just moved into a house. After you have finished reading, answer the questions that follow.

> *He was surprised to see a snake raise its head in the toilet bowl. He flushed the toilet and shortly thereafter it came up in the toilet across the hall. The police arrived and nothing happened. They suspected the man of being demented. But the second time they were called they found the snake. It was a five-foot boa constrictor. Apparently the former owner had tried to dispose of it by flushing it down the toilet. . . . Some good stories have no moral, but this story has one: Never flush a boa constrictor down a toilet.*
>
> from *"Snakes, Just Snakes" by Mrs. Kemper Campbell*

1. Do you think this is an informal or a formal essay? Explain your answer.

The essay is informal because it is funny and it sounds like the writer is talking to me.

2. How might the essay be different if the author had written it with another purpose in mind?

Students may suggest that if the essay were written formally they would not expect

the chatty tone and humorous details.

B. In your opinion, which detail in the excerpt is most memorable? Why? Explain how this detail helped you answer the questions in Section A above.

Students should cite a detail and explain why they found it memorable and how it

may have helped them answer the questions in Section A. For example, a humorous

detail would have helped them determine that the essay is informal.

To review

page 117

Main Idea and Details

| Lesson 14 | Introducing page 107 | Practicing page 108 | Applying page 109 | Reviewing page 119 | Testing page 120 |

Introducing Strategies

The **main idea** is the central, or most important, point that a writer wants to make. It is usually found at the beginning or the end of an essay. Main ideas can be stated directly. They can also be implied, which means that readers must figure out the main idea from the information given.

Writers use **details** to support their main idea. An individual paragraph within a larger piece of writing can also contain its own main idea and supporting details.

The diagram below shows you how details support or explain the main idea.

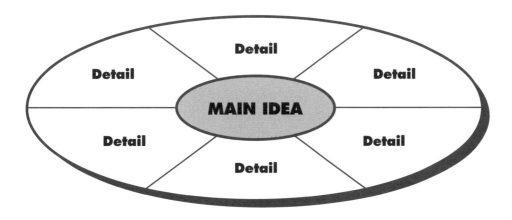

Reading the Essay

Reread "Why _Roots_ Is An Important Work to African Americans" on pages 110-112. Underline the main idea of the essay and circle the details that support it. Use these notes to answer the questions below.

1. What is the main idea of this essay?

The book _Roots_ helps African Americans value their families and their African

cultural heritage.

2. Describe one supporting detail in the essay. Then explain how it supports the main idea.

Accept all details from the essay if students connect them to the main idea identified

above. Many details are circled on pages 110-112.

Lesson Objective: To identify main idea and details in the essays "Why _Roots_ Is an Important Work to African Americans" and "Advertising."

ESL/LEP: Show pictures of African villages and cities from books. Ask students to identify what they see. Explain that these are details. Then help students invent a title for each picture.

Modeling the Strategy: Read aloud a passage from a nonfiction book to model finding main ideas and details. After completing the page, use the Reproducible Activity master on page T13 of the ATE to help students apply the strategy to "Why _Roots_ Is an Important Work to African Americans."

Managing the Lesson: Remind students that they can use the supporting details they circled and the main idea they underlined to help them answer questions 1 and 2.

Practicing *Main Idea and Details*

Purpose: The purpose of this page is to help students identify main ideas and details in an essay. Questions reflect the strategy illustrated in the diagram on the **Introducing** page.

A. Circle the letter of the item that best completes each statement below. Then, on the lines that follow it, write the main idea of the paragraph in your own words.

1. Winbush states, "The greatest success of *Roots* has been in making African Americans feel better about their cultural heritage." He supports this statement by pointing out that

    a. Alex Haley was an African American.

    b. fitting together a family history is hard work.

    c. the Africans in Haley's book were "smart, resourceful people."

    (d.) African Americans can understand more about themselves by understanding African culture.

The more African Americans understand their African heritage, the more proud they

become of their African American culture.

Peer Sharing: Have students complete Section A with a classmate. Both partners should be able to explain why they made the choices they did.

2. Which detail supports the main idea stated in #1 above?

    (a.) African Americans now appreciate the beauty of African names.

    b. Africans and African Americans share a love of music.

    c. Kunta Kinte was a smart, resourceful man.

    d. Slave masters did not value the lives of the African slaves.

This detail supports the main idea because it reflects a change that was inspired

by *Roots*.

Writing Process: Students may choose to develop their responses into full-length essays as a total writing process activity.

B. Do you think it is important to know about your heritage? State your opinion in your main idea and support it with details.

Students should state whether or not they think it is important to know about their

own heritage. This opinion should be supported by details. Students might refer to

ideas from the essay to defend their own thoughts.

_____

_____

_____

_____

_____

_____

Applying Main Idea and Details

A. Read the following excerpt from "The Stunt Pilot," an essay by Annie Dillard. This excerpt tells about a crop-duster pilot, someone who flies the plane that sprays fertilizer or pesticide on crops. The author considers these fliers to be stunt pilots. After you have finished reading, answer the questions below.

> *A crop-duster pilot in Wyoming told me the life expectancy of a crop-duster pilot is five years. They fly too low. They hit buildings and power lines. They have no space to fly out of trouble, and no space to recover from a stall. We were in Cody, Wyoming, out on the north fork of the Shoshone River. The crop duster had wakened me that morning flying over the ranch house and clearing my bedroom roof by half an inch. I saw the bolts on the wheel assembly a few feet from my face.*
>
> from *"The Stunt Pilot"* by Annie Dillard

1. On the lines below, write two details that support the statement that crop duster pilots have a very short life expectancy.

Students may list: They fly too low, they hit buildings and power lines, they cannot fly

out of trouble or recover from a stall.

2. What personal experience does the writer describe to help support the main idea of the excerpt?

The author describes a time she saw a crop duster fly overhead on a ranch in

Cody, Wyoming.

B. Imagine that you think crop-duster pilots have a safe job. Rewrite the paragraph using this as your main idea. Add details to support it.

Students' main idea should support the argument that crop dusters have safe jobs.

They should support the stated idea with invented details.

_____

_____

_____

_____

Applying the Skill to Everyday Reading: Students can practice identifying main ideas and details in articles they read in the school or local newspaper.

Prior Knowledge: Have students locate Wyoming on a map. Ask them to locate other states in which people have ranches.

Cooperative Learning: Have students complete the page in groups of three. One student should be the reader, another the moderator, and the third the recorder. Students may enjoy comparing their responses to Section B.

Assessing Cooperative Work: As you observe groups, note the degree to which members listen to one another, contribute to the discussion, and add relevant information. Then have individual members rate themselves.

To review

↓

page 119

The author wants to tell the reader about *Roots,* a book based on African American history. He may be trying to introduce a serious topic here.

So far, this essay shows how the book *Roots* is related to African American history. The writer is very serious about this subject, so this may be a formal essay.

I know that formal essays don't usually give personal information about the writer. So far, Donald E. Winbush hasn't added any personal information.

Donald E. Winbush is an Atlanta-based speechwriter, journalist, and creative writer. As a professor at Clark Atlanta University, he has helped other African Americans develop their skills as journalists. He has contributed to many national publications and television news programs.

Why *Roots* Is an Important Work to African Americans

by Donald E. Winbush

Some books that teach important lessons are also fun to read. One such book is *Roots* by Alex Haley. *Roots* is one of the most important history books ever written for African Americans. It can help African Americans to understand how strong and valuable their families are. It also reveals the beauty of African cultural heritage.

When *Roots* was first published, some people thought it was too long and too hard to read. That is not the case. The book *is* 688 pages long and is very well written. Alex Haley had a gift for storytelling. He made his characters seem like everyday people.

Others said the popular TV movie *Roots* was more important than Alex Haley's book. However, without the book, the movie would not have been possible.

One of the great lessons of *Roots* is that African Americans can, and should, learn more about their families. Because of slavery, this knowledge is especially important for African Americans. Many families were torn apart by slavery. Slave masters insisted that the lives of African Americans were not worth much—although the masters did benefit greatly from the work done by the enslaved people.

Roots shows African Americans that learning about family histories can help fit families together—like working a puzzle. The book follows the life of Kunta Kinte, an African boy who was captured and enslaved. It also traces the lives of Kunta Kinte's relatives in the United States. The family includes enslaved people, formerly enslaved people, farmers, architects, lawyers, and, of course, Alex Haley.

Inspired by *Roots,* many African Americans have explored their own family histories. Like Haley, they have discovered many success stories. They have learned about relatives who had unusual personalities and who accomplished remarkable things. They are impressed by the ways their families overcame slavery and other hardships. This information has helped African Americans feel proud to be part of a unique group. It inspires many to greater achievements of their own.

Digging up family history and fitting together the pieces is hard work. It's like being a detective. Alex Haley spent ten years researching and writing *Roots*. To help other African Americans with their own investigations, Haley offers this important clue: Among the best sources of information are the oldest living members of a family.

Family stories told by his grandmother were the spark that made Haley want to search for his family's roots. In following Haley's lead, many other African Americans have been pleading with their family elders to tell stories about the old days. Hearing stories from the older folks is important. There are not many written histories of African American families.

The greatest success of *Roots* has been in making African Americans feel better about their cultural heritage. This is important because how African Americans talk, dress, and live is connected to Africa. By understanding more about African culture, African Americans understand more about themselves.

Before *Roots*, some African Americans believed that Africa was a dull place. They believed that African people were not smart and that they led boring lives. For African Americans to think that way about their own cultural heritage was tragic.

Roots did as much as any other book ever published to change those negative feelings. The book is filled with stories about Kunta Kinte and other members of Alex Haley's family. It shows Africans as smart, resourceful people. They had great dignity and led fascinating lives.

For example, one part of *Roots* tells how Kunta Kinte and other African boys, beginning at 10 years old, went through "manhood training." They were taken from their villages to a special place and taught to be good hunters and warriors. They also learned that being a man meant being honest. Manhood training was a proud and important African tradition. Yet it was one that few African Americans were aware of.

Roots also made African Americans appreciate the beauty of African names. Many had thought that names from Africa sounded strange. *Roots* revealed how important names and their meanings are to Africans. As a result, many African American parents have given their

◄ If this essay were informal, it would most likely be funny in places. So far, the author is explaining information that is not humorous.

◄ The author and Alex Haley believe people should look to their family elders to discover their family histories. Now that's something for me to think about.

Clarification: You may wish to have students reread up to this paragraph to clarify that the experience of enslavement led many African Americans to feel their cultural heritage should be forgotten.

◄ As I continue to read, I'll watch for whether the author continues to discuss his topic in a serious tone.

As you read, write your owns notes about formal and informal essays in the margins.

Cultural Awareness: Have students list any other names they know that come from African or other cultures.

children beautiful African names like Omari, which means "the highest," or Lulu, which means "a pearl." Some parents have named their children Kunta, after the main character in *Roots*. Often, at family reunions, African Americans sport colorful T-shirts that show names of family members who lived in Africa many, many years ago. *Roots* inspired the detective work and pride that makes those T-shirts meaningful.

Without *Roots*, many African Americans would never have appreciated Africa's influence on their own lives. Here is one example. While he was writing *Roots*, Alex Haley traveled several times to Africa. Stories about his experiences stirred strong feelings in African Americans.

In one story, Haley told about trying to convince an African guide to take him to a faraway village. The guide was tired and did not want to make the journey. No matter how hard he tried, Haley could not change the travel guide's mind.

Finally, the guide agreed to go with Haley. But he insisted that he had to bring one other person along. He told Haley that he absolutely had to bring along the village music man, who would make the journey more pleasurable for them both.

When African Americans heard that story, they often did something very surprising. They sprang suddenly to their feet and cheered and clapped their hands wildly. What made them so emotional? It was because the story helped them to understand a strong cultural connection. Just as music was important to Africans, it is important in the lives of African Americans.

With a powerful family story, *Roots* gives African Americans the greatest lesson ever about their proud and priceless heritage. No work has done more to explain and celebrate Africa and her cultures. Truly, *Roots* is a treasure of strength and dignity to millions of Americans who had never before felt good about their history.

Response Clue: Students may note that formal essays may include personal information, but that their tone is not chatty.

ESL/LEP: Help students understand the meaning of the idiom *change his mind*.

Summarizing: Have students stop and summarize the main idea of the material they have read and comment on the style in which the essay was written.

If you are working on

Lesson 13 | Lesson 14

↓ | ↓

page 104 | page 107

Andrew A. Rooney's work is featured weekly on the television program *60 Minutes*, where, in the feature "A Few Minutes with Andy Rooney," he reads essays similar to this one. He began writing for *Stars and Stripes*, the magazine of the United States Armed Services, during World War II and has since won many awards for his work.

Advertising

by Andrew A. Rooney

My grandfather told me when I was a small boy that if a product was any good, they shouldn't have to advertise it.

I believed my grandfather at the time, but then years later my mother said that when *she* was a little girl he had told her that they'd never be able to build an automobile that would go up a hill. So I never knew whether to believe my grandfather or not.

Like so many things, I've really never made up my mind about advertising. I know all the arguments for it and against it, but the one thing I'm sure of is that there ought to be some sanctuaries, some places we're safe from being advertised at. There ought to be some open space left in the world without any advertising on it, some pieces of paper, some painted surfaces that aren't covered with entreaties for us to buy something. Advertising doesn't belong on license plates, for instance. Of the fifty states, twenty-seven of them have slogans trying to sell themselves to the rest of us. It's offensive and wrong. The license plate has an important function and it's a cheap trick to tack something else on it. Most of the legends the states put on aren't true anyway.

Rhode Island, for instance, says it's the "Ocean State." There are fifteen states with more ocean than Rhode Island has. If they want to say something on their plate, why don't they explain why they call Rhode an island when it isn't one?

Florida says it's the "Sunshine State." I like Florida, but why don't they also say that Miami has more rain than any city in the whole United States except for Mobile, Alabama?

North Carolina says it's "First in Freedom." It doesn't say anywhere on the license plate who they think is *second* in freedom. South Carolina? Michigan?

Connecticut says it's the "Constitution State." I called the license bureau in Connecticut and no one there could tell me why they call it the Constitution State. Connecticut is not the Constitution state, of course. *Pennsylvania* is the Constitution state. And Pennsylvania calls itself the "Keystone State." Does anyone really care?

Maine says it's "Vacationland." How would you like to drive a garbage truck for eight hours in Augusta with a sign hanging on the back that says "Vacationland"? . . .

New Mexico calls itself "Land of Enchantment." This is not the kind of slogan that gets the work of the world done. . . .

Wisconsin "America's Dairyland"? Never mind that, Wisconsin, if you're dairyland why don't you tell us on your license plates what ever happened to heavy cream? That's the kind of stuff we'd like to read about when we're driving along behind a car from your state.

And then Idaho. How would you like to work hard, save your money and decide, when the kids were educated and the house paid for, to buy a Mercedes-Benz. You plunk down your $28,000, the dealer screws on the license plate and there you are with your dream car, you drive away, and affixed to the bumper is the sign that says "Famous Potatoes."

"If a state is any good," I imagine my grandfather would have said, "it shouldn't have to advertise."

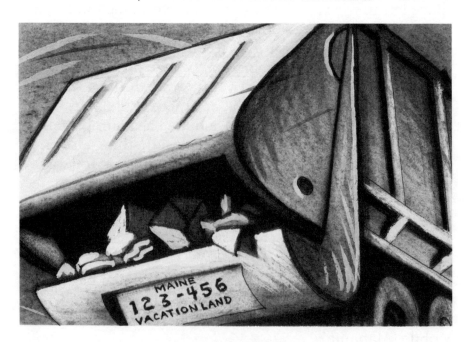

License-plate advertising is a small part of what we're faced with when we're driving. On the highways, trucks are turned into rolling billboards. The companies that own them look on it as easy advertising, too cheap to pass up. On major highways the commercials come along more often than on a late-night television movie.

On city streets, the billboards on Coca-Cola and Pepsi trucks are often double-parked while the driver makes deliveries. In most cities now, taxis and buses carry advertising. When you're paying a buck and a half a mile, you shouldn't have to carry a sign pushing cigarettes.

In California there's a company called Beetleboards. What Beetleboards will do for you is paint your Volkswagen, apply a commercial motif from a sponsor who is paying them and pay you twenty dollars a month to drive around in it.

And if you can understand businesses advertising their products on our roads, how do you account for the private citizens who use the back end of their cars to tell us about themselves or about some private campaign of theirs? A typical car or van in a parking lot outside a tourist attraction in Washington, D.C., will announce through the decals attached to it somewhere, that the owner is insured by Allstate, boosts the Northern Virginia Ramparts—a team of some sort, I guess—is against forest fires because he has a little Smokey the Bear stuck to his car, gives to the International Convention of Police Chiefs and believes in God because his bumper sticker tells us so.

If someone has to take pride in having people know what insurance company gets his money, he's in trouble for things to be proud of.

A third of the cars on the road have reading matter stuck to them somewhere trying to sell the rest of us a place, an opinion or a way of life. Sometimes it looks as though half the cars in the United States have been to a roadside stand in South Carolina called South of the Border, and for some reason the entrepreneurs who have made tourist attractions out of caves love to slap "Visit Secret Caverns" on visitors' bumpers.

One of the most incredible commercial coups of the century has been pulled off by the designers who have conned women into thinking it's chic to wear a piece of apparel on which the maker's name is imprinted as part of the design.

The French luggage maker Louis Vuitton may have started the trend when he made the brown LV the only

ESL/LEP: Help students understand the meaning of the idiom *too cheap to pass up*.

Clarification: You may wish to have students reread this paragraph to clarify that the word *Beetleboards* relates to Volkswagen cars. The word *beetle* was a nickname for this make of car.

Cultural Awareness: Have students describe bumper stickers they have seen. Encourage them to discuss what they might learn about a culture from its bumper stickers.

Response Clue: Students may now understand that this humorous paragraph supports the idea that there is too much advertising.

Response Clue: Students may identify the circled sentences as details that support the main idea that there should be some places that are free from advertising.

Summarizing: Have students summarize the main ideas and supporting details they have read as well as the style with which these ideas and details are presented.

Meeting Individual Needs: Some students might need help understanding the humor in this paragraph. Rooney is comparing being overwhelmed with advertising to being hunted like a deer.

Response Clue: Ask students to compare the idea expressed in the last sentence with the idea expressed in the first two paragraphs of the essay. They may develop a sidenote pointing out that the concluding sentence restates the main idea.

design on his product, but the women's fashion designers have taken it over. Bill Blass makes towels with his name all over them. Why would anyone want to take a shower and buff themselves dry on a piece of cloth bearing Bill Blass's name? . . .

Why would I or anyone else want to lay me down to sleep with my head on a pillowcase embossed with the signature of Yves Saint Laurent?

The first time I remember seeing a designer's name on something, the name was Pucci. It seemed amusing enough but now they're all doing it. Halston, Calvin Klein and Diane Von Furstenberg must all be wonderfully famous and talented, but if I buy anything of theirs I'd prefer to have it anonymous. If I got a scarf with Diane Von Furstenberg's name on it, which is unlikely, my first inclination would be to send it out to the cleaners to have them try to get it out.

The advertisers are coming at us from all directions all the time. If we were deer, a closed season would be declared on us to protect an endangered species. It just seems wrong to me that we're spending more time and money trying to sell some things than we are making them in the first place. I'm an all-American consumer but there are just certain times and places I don't want to be sold anything.

If you are working on

Lesson 13	Lesson 14
⬇	⬇
page 117	page 119

Reviewing *Reading Essays*

A. Read "Advertising" on pages 113-116. While you read, use the wide margin to take notes to help you decide if this is a formal or an informal essay. Then use the checklist below to organize your ideas.

Reviewing the Strategy: Have students refer to the sidenotes they wrote on pages 113-116. Tell them to use their notes to help them check the appropriate boxes on the essay checklist.

ESSAY CHECKLIST

Informal Essay

- ☑ informal tone (sounds as if the writer is chatting with the reader)
- ☑ the writer tells something about himself or herself
- ☑ may contain humor
- ☑ purpose is to entertain

Formal Essay

- ☐ serious tone, not humorous
- ☐ carefully organized, not rambling or chatty
- ☐ not much personal information
- ☐ purpose is to discuss a serious topic

B. Answer the questions below. Use your sidenotes and the details in the checklist above to help you.

1. Is this essay informal or formal? Give reasons for your answer.

The essay is informal; students may use any of the characteristics listed in the

Informal Essays section of the checklist to support their choice.

Managing the Lesson: Answers on the checklist are suggestions. Students may note that this essay also contains characteristics of formal essays. They should be able to support their choices.

2. Make up a slogan for license plates in your state and tell why you chose it. Your slogan can be either serious or funny.

Students may make up serious or funny slogans for state license plates. Check to see

that an explanation for the slogan has been given.

Writing Process: Students might choose to develop their writing into the first draft of an informal or formal essay.

Testing Reading Essays

A. Fill in the bubble next to each true statement. Then, on the lines provided, explain your answer.

1. ● "Advertising" is an informal essay.

The essay is informal because it contains personal information and humor

and is chatty.

2. ○ We don't learn anything about the personal life and thoughts of Andrew A. Rooney in the essay.

The author speaks about himself and his past experiences with advertising.

3. ● The author writes as if he is carrying on a conversation with the reader.

The tone is informal, like a chat between the author and the reader.

4. ○ The writer of "Advertising" is serious at all times.

The writer makes jokes about places where advertisements are found.

B. On the lines below, write an essay discussing your ideas about advertising. Use either a formal or an informal tone.

Students should state a main idea about advertising at the beginning of the essay.

A main idea for each paragraph should be supported by details. The tone—either

formal or informal—should be maintained throughout the essay.

To begin
Lesson 14

page
107

Reviewing Main Idea and Details

A. Reread "Advertising" on pages 113-116. As you read, underline the main idea of the essay and circle the supporting details. Then use the chart below to record your findings.

Reviewing the Strategy: Have students refer to the circled details and underlined main ideas they noted on pages 113-116. Tell them to write the main idea in the center circle. They should write a supporting detail in each of the sections surrounding this circle.

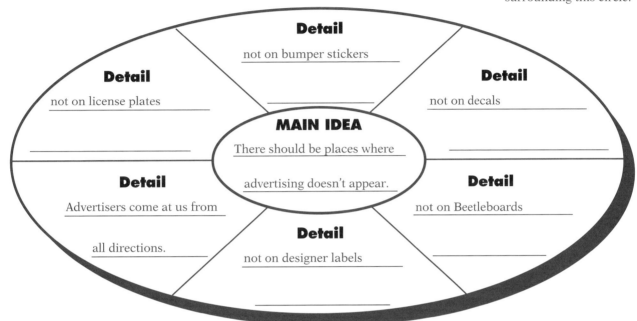

Detail
not on bumper stickers

Detail
not on license plates

Detail
not on decals

MAIN IDEA
There should be places where advertising doesn't appear.

Detail
Advertisers come at us from all directions.

Detail
not on Beetleboards

Detail
not on designer labels

Managing the Lesson: Answers on the wheel are suggestions. Students may list other details.

B. Do you agree or disagree with Andrew A. Rooney's opinion about designer names on clothing and other items? Write a paragraph in which you state your opinion, or main idea, in the first sentence. Make sure your paragraph includes at least three supporting details.

Students should clearly state their opinions at the beginning of their paragraphs. They should include three supporting details and a concluding sentence.

Cooperative Learning: Have students complete the page in groups of three. One student should be the reader, another the moderator, and the third the recorder. Invite groups to debate their ideas.

Testing Main Idea and Details

A. For each item below, read the sentence from the essay. Then read the two statements that follow it and circle the true statement. (In some items, both statements are true.) Explain your choice on the lines that follow.

1. "You plunk down your $28,000, the dealer screws on the license plate and there you are with your dream car, you drive away, and affixed to the bumper is the sign that says 'famous potatoes.'"

   a. This sentence supports the main idea of the essay: that advertising does not belong on license plates.

   (b.) This sentence supports the main idea of the essay: that some places should be free of advertising.

   The main idea of the essay is that some places should be free from advertising; that

   advertising does not belong on license plates is a detail.

2. "Advertising doesn't belong on license plates. . . ."

   (a.) This sentence states the main idea of one paragraph.

   b. This statement supports the main idea of one paragraph.

   This is the main idea of one paragraph. It is supported by descriptions of license

   plates from several states.

3. "License-plate advertising is a small part of what we're faced with when we're driving."

   (a.) This sentence is supported by the statement that trucks are covered with advertising.

   (b.) This sentence is supported by a description of different types of bumper stickers.

   The sentence is the main idea of a paragraph. It is supported by details about

   advertising on trucks.

B. Do you think advertisers should be allowed to advertise everywhere? Provide details that support your answer.

Students should state their opinion clearly at the beginning of the paragraph, provide

supporting details, and finish with a concluding sentence.

_____

_____

_____

_____

Book Test

PART 1: FICTION

Read the story below and respond to it by underlining key ideas and writing notes in the margins. Then use the story and your notes to answer the questions on the next page.

The Wig

1 Everyone loved Carla's naturally curly hair. Everyone, that is, except Carla. On one really horrible bad hair day, Carla's older sister Maureen offered to help. She would put a chemical straightener on Carla's hair.

2 The results were shocking. Carla's hair stuck straight out in all directions. "What am I going to do?" cried Carla. "I can't go to school like this. I look like a clown!"

3 "Maybe a haircut will help," suggested her mother. Carla cried all the way to the beauty shop. The hair stylist tried, but nothing worked. Carla's hair was fried.

4 "Mom," Carla cried, "I have to get a wig."

5 After Carla wore her new wig to school for a few weeks, everyone stopped talking about it. Everyone that is, except Mrs. Prince, the gym teacher. One of Mrs. Prince's rules was that girls with hair longer than their chin had to wear a headband. Carla's wig was just short of her chin. So she was surprised when Mrs. Prince said, "Your hair is getting long, Carla. I think you should start wearing a headband."

6 The next day, Carla's team was playing baseball. When it was her turn to bat, Carla walked with confidence to the plate. She was the best hitter on her team. Jason, the most popular boy in her high school, was pitching.

7 She calmly pushed her headband up out of her eyes. Then a terrible thing happened. The wig came off in her hands. There she stood with her three frizzy ponytails.

8 Carla dashed behind the bleachers. As she ran, she could tell that Mrs. Prince was trying hard not to laugh.

9 "It is pretty funny," Carla thought, as she stuffed the three stiff ponytails under the wig. "But *now* what am I going to do?"

10 Gathering her strength, she walked out from behind the bleachers. "I guess I'm up," she said with a smile.

11 Jason gave her a little smile and threw her a pitch.

12 The next day Carla decided to leave her wig at home.

Lesson Management: You may want to use the Book Tests as pretests or posttests to assess students' reading comprehension. The skills tested in Part 1 include: recognizing fantasy, plot, multiple meaning words, base words and affixes, sequence, cause and effect, and making inferences.

Alternative Assessment: Students' notations and text markings will reflect their familiarity with active reading skills. Rank the students' notes and text markings based on the following criteria to assess their application of the skills and strategies taught in *Crossroads*: *0*: No response; *1*: Markings and notes consistently inappropriate; *2*: Partially appropriate markings or notes; *3*: Appropriate markings with some unclear notes; *4*: Appropriate markings and clear notes; *5*: Exceptional markings and notes.

A. Use the story and your notes to identify the best answer to each question below. Ask students to provide evidence that supports each response.

1. Which detail shows that this story is NOT a fantasy?
- a. Carla's hair turns gold.
- b. Carla's hair immediately returns to normal.
- c. Carla's hair sticks out in all directions.
- d. Carla's hair obeys her wishes.

recognizing fantasy

2. What is the MAIN conflict in the story?
- a. Carla tries not to be angry with her sister.
- b. Carla doesn't like her curly hair.
- c. Carla tries to wear a wig in her gym class.
- d. Carla's gym teacher wants students to follow rules.

plot

3. Which definition of *shop* matches how the word is used in paragraph 3?
- a. a store
- b. to buy goods from a store
- c. a place where goods are produced
- d. a place where a service is provided

multiple meaning words

4. This line appears paragraph 6: "Carla walked with confidence to the plate." What is the BEST meaning of the suffix *-ed* in the word *walked*?
- a. something that is happening now
- b. something that will happen
- c. something that happened in the past
- d. something that may happen

base words and affixes

5. After Carla tucks her ponytails under the wig in paragraph 9, she
- a. runs behind the bleachers.
- b. cries, "I look like a clown!"
- c. has her hair cut.
- d. gathers her strength and walks up to bat.

sequence

6. Carla begins wearing a wig because
- a. she is tired of having straight hair.
- b. her hair has been ruined by a chemical straightener.
- c. her gym teacher tells her that her hair is too long.
- d. she wants curly hair.

cause and effect

B. At the end of the story, Carla decides not to wear her wig to school. Write a paragraph that explains Carla's decision. Use story evidence and what you already know to make your inferences.
making inferences

Students may suggest: Carla decides not to wear her wig anymore because she realizes that it is not how her hair

looks that will make people like her, but how she acts and who she is. In addition, the fact that her classmates

don't tease her helps her self-esteem. As a result, she stops focusing on her hair and tries not to be perfect.

Book Test

PART 2: NONFICTION

Read the following speech, which was presented by an environmentalist at a high school in Los Angeles. Draw arrows to show related ideas and write notes in the margins as you respond to the speech. Then use the speech and your notes to answer the questions on the next page.

You Can Make a Difference

1 Vice-President Gore often tells a true story about a frog that was put into a pot of water. The water was slowly heated until it boiled. But even though it was able to do so, the frog did not jump out of the water.

2 According to the vice-president, many people are like that frog. They close their eyes to the changes in the environment. Although we are poisoning ourselves, many people, like the frog, are doing nothing about it.

3 You and I can choose to be different. We can choose to hop out of that pot. We can take a stand. We can make choices that will help protect the environment.

4 Did you know that one quart of oil can actually pollute two million gallons of water? If your family puts its used motor oil in a hazardous waste dump, you can protect two million gallons of water. Better yet, your family can recycle your motor oil so that it could be used again.

5 If you turn off the lights in your house when they are not needed, you can help prevent acid rain. As you probably know, acid rain is caused by air pollution. A light bulb actually gives off gases that cause acid rain.

6 There are other ways that you can help decrease air pollution. You can ride a bike or walk when you are going a short distance. Use a car only for longer trips.

7 Did you know that a typical family of four throws out 200 large garbage cans of trash each year? This trash has to go somewhere. But we are running out of room for it.

8 Much of the trash that is going to landfills—areas set aside for garbage—can be recycled. Bottles, paper, cans, and many metals are recyclable. If you and your family recycle these materials, you can cut your trash in half.

9 So you see, one person can make a difference. We do not have to act like frogs, waiting to be boiled.

Lesson Management:
You may want to use the Book Tests as pretests or posttests to assess students' reading comprehension. The skills tested in Part 2 include: author's purpose, main idea and details, structure of speeches, making judgments, reading essays, synonyms and antonyms, and author's viewpoint.

Alternative Assessment: Circulate among your students while they complete the test. Observe their reactions as they work. Then evaluate their notes and text markings to assess their ability to apply the skills and strategies taught in *Crossroads*. Students' notations and text markings will reflect their familiarity with active reading skills.

A. Use the speech and your notes to identify the best answer for each question below. Ask students to provide evidence that supports each response.

1. What is the author's purpose in this speech?
   a. to state facts about the environment
   b. to explain frog biology
   c. to persuade people to take care of the environment
   d. to persuade people to turn off lights

author's purpose

2. What is the main idea of paragraph 3?
   a. All people do not have to be and act the same.
   b. People can take a stand.
   c. People can choose to protect the environment.
   d. Changes are occurring in the environment.

main idea and details

3. Which paragraph focuses on things that people can do to help the environment?
   a. paragraph 1
   b. paragraph 3
   c. paragraph 6
   d. paragraph 9

structure of speeches

4. This line appears in paragraph 8: "Bottles, paper, cans, and many metals are recyclable." What type of statement is this?
   a. a fact
   b. an opinion
   c. a fact and an opinion
   d. neither a fact nor an opinion

making judgments

5. Which of the following tells you that "You Can Make a Difference" is a formal speech?
   a. It contains humor.
   b. It includes details about the author's life.
   c. The author seems to chat with the audience.
   d. The author takes her subject seriously.

reading essays

6. What is the BEST synonym for the word *recycle* in paragraph 4?
   a. throw away
   b. use again
   c. discard
   d. keep

synonyms and antonyms

B. Write a paragraph in which you compare the author's viewpoint about protecting the environment with your own viewpoint on this subject.
author's viewpoint

Students might agree with the author that people need to do something to protect the environment. They may

mention the following strategies: recycling oil, bottles, paper, cans, and many metals; turning off unnecessary

lights; riding a bike; and walking short distances instead of driving. They might also talk to others about their

concerns, organize groups to clean up parts of their community, and write to government officials about

industrial pollution.